THE CALIFORNIA DIRECTORY OF
FIN·E WINERIES

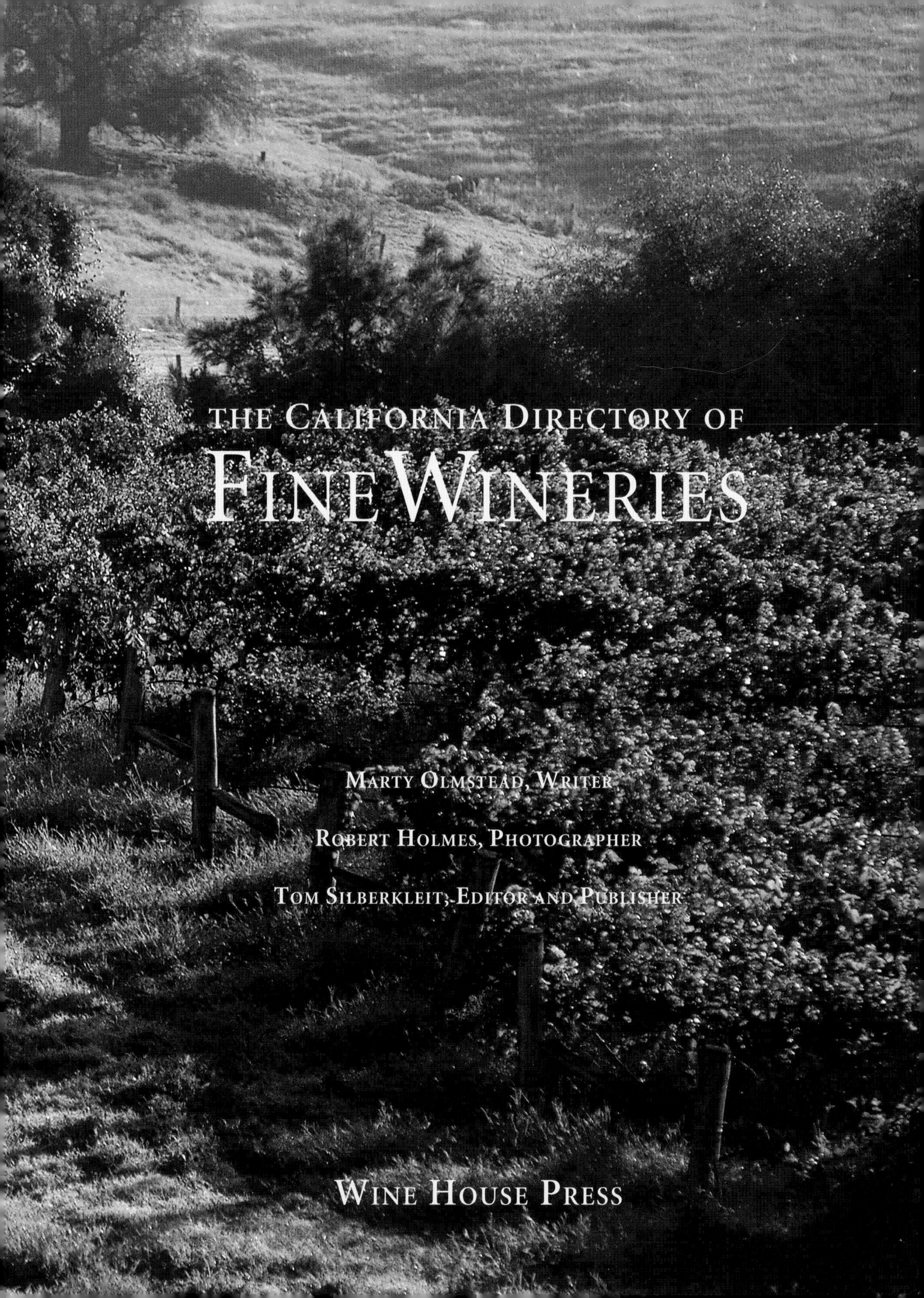

THE CALIFORNIA DIRECTORY OF
FINE WINERIES

MARTY OLMSTEAD, WRITER

ROBERT HOLMES, PHOTOGRAPHER

TOM SILBERKLEIT, EDITOR AND PUBLISHER

WINE HOUSE PRESS

CONTENTS

INTRODUCTION 7

READING A WINE LABEL 8

WHAT IS AN APPELLATION? 9

NAPA WINERIES 11

Artesa Vineyards and Winery
Beaulieu Vineyards
Beringer Vineyards
Cakebread Cellars
Chimney Rock Winery
Domaine Carneros
Duckhorn Vineyards
Edgewood Estate Winery

Flora Springs Winery and
   Vineyards
Franciscan Oakville Estate
Freemark Abbey Winery
Grgich Hills Cellar
Heitz Wine Cellars
The Hess Collection Winery
Joseph Phelps Vineyards

Markham Vineyards
Mumm Napa Valley
Niebaum-Coppola Estate
   Winery
Robert Mondavi Winery
Rutherford Hill Winery
Silver Oak Cellars
Silverado Vineyards

St. Clement Vineyards
St. Supéry Vineyards and
   Winery
Sterling Vineyards
Swanson Vineyards and
   Winery
William Hill Winery
ZD Wines

SONOMA WINERIES 71

Alderbrook Vineyards and
   Winery
Arrowood Vineyards &
   Winery
Benziger Family Winery
Buena Vista Carneros Estate
   Winery
Chateau Souverain Winery
Chateau St. Jean Winery

Cline Cellars
Davis Bynum Winery
Fritz Winery
Gloria Ferrer Champagne
   Caves
Imagery Estate Winery
J Vineyards and Winery
Kenwood Vineyards
Landmark Vineyards

Ledson Winery and
   Vineyards
Matanzas Creek Winery and
   Estate Gardens
Mazzocco Vineyards
Ravenswood Winery
Raymond Burr Vineyards
Schug Carneros Estate
   Winery

Sebastiani Vineyards and
   Winery
Simi Winery
St. Francis Winery &
   Vineyards
Stone Creek Wines
Viansa Winery & Italian
   Marketplace

MENDOCINO WINERIES 125

Barra of Mendocino
Brutocao Cellars
Fetzer Vineyards
Frey Vineyards, Ltd.
Handley Cellars
Milano Family Winery
Roederer Estate

ACKNOWLEDGMENTS 143

INTRODUCTION

Whether you are a visitor or a native seeking the ultimate chalice of nectar from the grape, navigating Northern California's wine country can be intimidating. Hundreds of wineries—from glamorous estates to converted barns, from nationally recognized labels to hidden gems—are found throughout Napa, Sonoma, and Mendocino. The challenge is deciding where to go and how to plan a trip. This book will be your indispensable traveling companion.

The sixty wineries in *The California Directory of Fine Wineries* are known for producing some of the world's most admired wines. From the moment you walk in the door of these wineries, you will be greeted like a guest and invited to sample at a relaxing, leisurely tempo. Although the quality of the winemaker's art is of paramount importance, the wineries are also notable as tourist destinations. Many boast award-winning contemporary architecture, while others are housed in lovingly preserved historical structures. Some have galleries featuring museum-quality artwork by local and international artists or exhibits focusing on the region's past and the history of winemaking. You will also enjoy taking informative behind-the-scenes tours, exploring inspirational gardens, and participating in celebrated culinary programs.

As you explore this magnificent region, you'll encounter some of California's most appealing scenery and attractions—mountain ranges, rugged coastline, pastures with majestic oak trees, abundant parkland, renowned spas, and historic towns. Use the information in this book to plan your trip, and be sure to stop along the way and take in the sights. You have my promise that traveling to your destination will be as sweet as the wine tasted upon your welcome.

—Tom Silberkleit
Editor and Publisher
Wine House Press
Sonoma, California

Reading a Wine Label

When you encounter an unfamiliar bottle of wine, you can learn a lot about it from inspecting the label. Federal law requires wineries to print specific information on the front label of each bottle. Some wineries include details on how a wine was made or how well it will pair with specific foods, usually on a separate label on the back of the bottle.

Most prominently displayed on the label is the name of the winery or the brand name. Also given emphasis is the type of wine. In most cases, this is the grape varietal, such as Chardonnay or Zinfandel. To carry the name of a varietal, the wine must be made of 75 percent of that varietal. Wineries can also use a generic name or a proprietary one such as Joseph Phelps Vineyards' Insignia.

NAME OF WINERY OR BRAND NAME — CHATEAU ST JEAN — VINTAGE — 1999 — Robert Young Vineyard — INDIVIDUAL VINEYARD — TYPE OF WINE — CHARDONNAY — PLACE OF ORIGIN — ALEXANDER VALLEY — ALCOHOL CONTENT — ALC 14.4% BY VOL

The place of origin on the label tells you where the grapes were grown, not necessarily where the wine was made. A label bearing the name "California" means that 100 percent of the grapes were grown within the state. To use a county name, 75 percent of the grapes must come from that county. To use an American Viticultural Area (AVA) or appellation, 85 percent of the grapes must come from the defined area. The vintage is the year the grapes were harvested, not the year the wine was released. The wine must contain at least 95 percent of the stated vintage. Labels sometimes identify an individual vineyard. This a way for the winemaker to indicate that the grapes came from an exceptional source. To be a vineyard-designated wine, a minimum of 95 percent of the grapes must have come from the vineyard named.

Any wine with an alcohol content of more than 14 percent must carry this information. Wines designated as "Table Wine," with 7 to 14 percent alcohol content, are not required to state such information. American-made wine that contains sulfites must say so on the front or back label. Sulfur dioxide is a natural by-product of winemaking. Some wineries also add sulfites as a preservative.

Other information found on labels may include the description "estate bottled." This tells you that the winery owns (or controls) the vineyard where the grapes were grown. A bottle labeled "reserve" indicates that the wine is of a superior quality compared with the winery's nonreserve offerings.

Labels for sparkling wines may contain the term *méthode champenoise*. The most salient feature of this process is allowing the wine to ferment for a second time inside the bottle, resulting in bubbles that are finer than those in sparkling wine made by other methods. Vintage sparkling wines are designated either regular vintage or *prestige cuvée* (also called *tête de cuvée* or premium vintage), meaning that the wine is the top of the line.

WHAT IS AN APPELLATION?

People who make, market, or consume fine wines often use the word *appellation* to refer to the geographical area where the grapes were grown. Inclusion of the appellation on the bottle label means that 85 percent of the wine is from that area.

The terms "appellation of origin" and "American Viticultural Area" (AVA) are frequently used interchangeably in casual conversation, but they are not synonymous. In the United States, appellations follow geopolitical borders, such as state and county lines, rather than geographic boundaries. AVAs are defined by such natural features as soil types, climate, and topography.

Since 1978, the U.S. Bureau of Alcohol, Tobacco and Firearms has been the arbiter of what does and does not qualify as an AVA. If a winery or group of wineries wants a particular area to qualify as an official AVA, they must prove that it has specific attributes that distinguish it significantly from its neighbors.

Why do winemakers care about this distinction? It is far more prestigious—and informative—to belong to an appellation such as Sonoma Valley, Napa Valley, or Russian River Valley than the more generic California, which means the grapes could have come from the Central Valley or anywhere else in the state. Informed consumers learn that a Chardonnay from the Alexander Valley, for instance, is apt to taste different from one originating in the Russian River Valley.

It's worth noting that a winery may be located in one appellation but use grapes from another to make a particular wine. In that case, the appellation used would be that of the source. For example, Ledson Winery and Vineyards is in the Sonoma Valley but makes a Pinot Noir using grapes from the Russian River Valley. Thus the bottle is labeled "Ledson Winery and Vineyards Pinot Noir, Russian River Valley."

The following are the appellations in Napa, Sonoma, and Mendocino:

NAPA	SONOMA	MENDOCINO
Atlas Peak	Alexander Valley	Anderson Valley
Carneros	Carneros	Cole Ranch
Chiles Valley District	Chalk Hill	McDowell Valley
Howell Mountain	Dry Creek Valley	Mendocino
Mount Veeder	Green Valley	Mendocino Ridge
Napa Valley	Knight's Valley	Potter Valley
Oakville	Northern Sonoma	Redwood Valley
Rutherford	Rockpile	Sanel Valley (proposed viticultural area)
St. Helena	Russian River Valley	Ukiah Valley (proposed viticultural area)
Spring Mountain District	Sonoma Coast	Yorkville Highlands (approval pending)
Stags Leap District	Sonoma Mountain	
Wild Horse Valley	Sonoma Valley	
Yountville		

NAPA

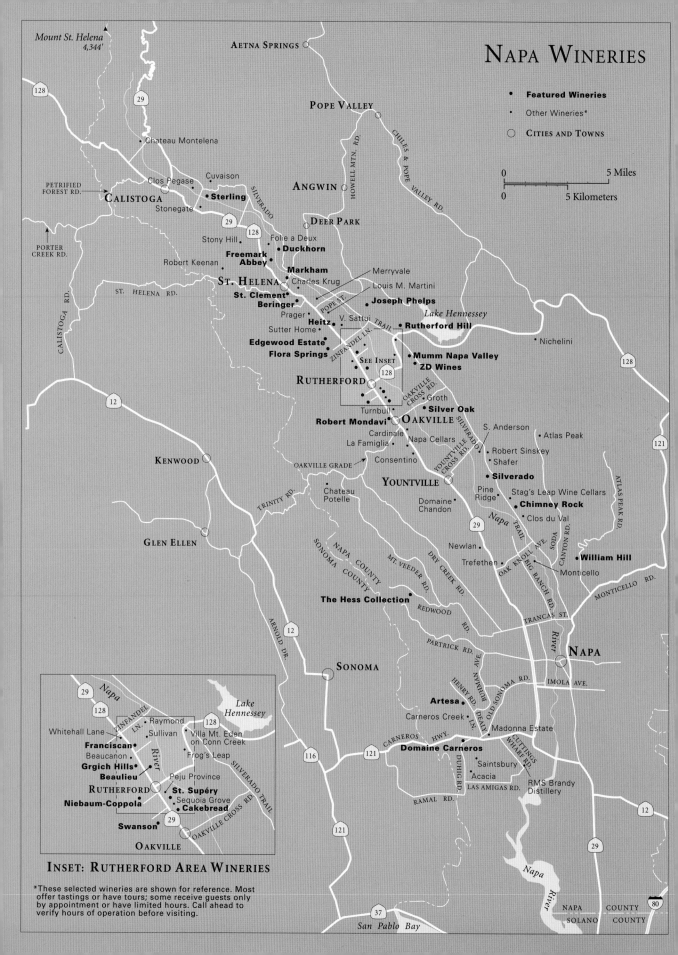

NAPA WINERIES

- ● **Featured Wineries**
- • Other Wineries*
- ○ CITIES AND TOWNS

0 _____ 5 Miles
0 _____ 5 Kilometers

Mount St. Helena
4,344'

AETNA SPRINGS

POPE VALLEY

128

29

ANGWIN

HOWELL MTN. RD.

CHILES & POPE VALLEY RD.

• Chateau Montelena

Clos Pegase • Cuvaison

PETRIFIED
FOREST RD.

CALISTOGA

Stonegate ●

● **Sterling**

SILVERADO

DEER PARK

29

PORTER
CREEK RD.

Stony Hill • Folie a Deux
● **Duckhorn**

128

Robert Keenan • ● **Freemark**
Abbey

CALISTOGA RD.

ST. HELENA RD.

ST. HELENA

● **Markham**
• Charles Krug

Merryvale
Louis M. Martini

● **St. Clement**
● **Beringer**
Prager •
● **Heitz**
Sutter Home •

POPE ST.

V. SATTUI TRAIL

● **Joseph Phelps**

Lake Hennessey

● **Rutherford Hill**

● **Edgewood Estate**
● **Flora Springs**

ZINFANDEL LN.

SEE INSET

● **Mumm Napa Valley**
● **ZD Wines**

• Nichelini

128

RUTHERFORD

128

• Groth
● **Silver Oak**

OAKVILLE CROSS RD.

Turnbull •
● **Robert Mondavi**

OAKVILLE

SILVERADO TRAIL

S. Anderson •

• Atlas Peak

121

Cardinale •
La Famiglia •
Napa Cellars •

Robert Sinskey •
• Shafer

ATLAS PEAK RD.

KENWOOD

OAKVILLE GRADE

Consentino •

YOUNTVILLE CROSS RD.

● **Silverado**

Pine
Ridge •

Stag's Leap Wine Cellars •
● **Chimney Rock**

TRINITY RD.

Chateau
Potelle •

YOUNTVILLE

Domaine
Chandon •

• Clos du Val

GLEN ELLEN

NAPA COUNTY

SONOMA COUNTY

MT. VEEDER RD.

DRY CREEK RD.

Napa
Trail

29

Newlan •
Trefethen •

OAK KNOLL AVE.

BIG RANCH RD.

SODA CANYON RD.

● **William Hill**
Monticello •

MONTICELLO RD.

ARNOLD DR.

12

● **The Hess Collection**

REDWOOD RD.

TRANCAS ST.

River

NAPA

SONOMA

PARTRICK RD.

HENRY RD.

BUHMAN LN.

DEALY LN.

OLD SONOMA RD.

IMOLA AVE.

● **Artesa**

Carneros Creek •

Madonna Estate •

CUTTINGS WHARF RD.

12

116

121

CARNEROS HWY.

● **Domaine Carneros**

Saintsbury •
Acacia •

DUHIG RD.

LAS AMIGAS RD.

RMS Brandy
Distillery •

121

RAMAL RD.

29

INSET: RUTHERFORD AREA WINERIES

29

Napa

128

ZINFANDEL LN.

• Raymond
• Sullivan

Whitehall Lane •

River

Lake
Hennessey

128

Villa Mt. Eden
on Conn Creek •

● **Franciscan**
Beaucanon •

Frog's Leap •

SILVERADO TRAIL

● **Grgich Hills**
● **Beaulieu**

Peju Province •

RUTHERFORD

● **St. Supéry**
Sequoia Grove •
● **Cakebread**

OAKVILLE CROSS RD.

● **Niebaum-Coppola**

29

● **Swanson** •

OAKVILLE

37

San Pablo Bay

Napa
River

NAPA   COUNTY
SOLANO COUNTY

80

*These selected wineries are shown for reference. Most
offer tastings or have tours; some receive guests only
by appointment or have limited hours. Call ahead to
verify hours of operation before visiting.

The most famous winemaking region in the United States, the Napa Valley is a microcosm of the wine country, with hundreds of wineries and thousands of acres of vineyards amassed in a narrow valley less than thirty miles long. This patchwork of agriculture extends north from upper San Pablo Bay to the dramatic palisades beside Calistoga. On the east, it is defined by a series of hills known as the Vaca Range. The western horizon is dominated  by the rugged peaks of the Mayacamas Range, including the steep inclines and forested slopes of Mount Veeder. The best way to get an overview is to take a hot-air balloon ride that departs at daybreak for a cool, calm flight above the vineyards and usually concludes with a champagne breakfast. The second-best way is to drive up the Oakville Grade and pull over at the top for a postcard-perfect view.

The county's largest cities are Napa and St. Helena, where you will find many shops and major attractions. Charming small towns along Highway 29, the main thoroughfare that is mostly only two lanes wide, have restaurants, inns, spas, and other businesses that cater to visitors.

ARTESA VINEYARDS AND WINERY

ARTESA VINEYARDS AND WINERY
1345 Henry Rd.
Napa, CA 94559
707-224-1668
info@artesawinery.com
www.artesawinery.com

OWNER: Codorniu.

LOCATION: About 7 miles southwest of the town of Napa.

APPELLATION: Carneros.

HOURS: 10 A.M.–5 P.M. daily.

TASTINGS: $6 for 6 wines; $8 for 4 reserve wines.

TOURS: 11 A.M. and 2 P.M.; self-guided tours during operating hours.

THE WINES: Cabernet Sauvignon, Chardonnay, late-harvest Gewürztraminer, Merlot, Pinot Noir, Sauvignon Blanc, sparkling wines, Syrah.

SPECIALTIES: Multiple bottlings of major varietals by appellation.

WINEMAKER: Don Van Staaveren.

ANNUAL PRODUCTION: 90,000 cases.

OF SPECIAL NOTE: Sparkling wine available only at winery; some limits on reserve wines. Art exhibitions and museum displays on local and European winemaking.

NEARBY ATTRACTIONS: di Rosa Preserve (indoor and outdoor exhibits of works by contemporary Bay Area artists).

Virtually the entire Carneros appellation is visible from this property, built into a hilltop in the southern Napa Valley. Despite this wraparound view, the winery itself is a more compelling vision. As visitors approach it, the entrance is hidden from sight. At the base of the staircase leading to Artesa, six abstract sculptures by artist-in-residence Gordon Huether encircle the main fountain. Only after mounting the steep double stairway to the plaza can visitors see the entry doors, dug into a hillside covered with native grasses. On this level are more fountains, spewing arches of water that collapse into tranquil pools. With its tiered construction, the winery is reminiscent of a hidden Mayan temple.

The modernist winery was designed by renowned Barcelona architect Domingo Triay and executed by Napa Valley architect Earl R. Bouligny. The 120,000-square-foot structure was created by removing 30 feet of hilltop and then matching the facility's height to the original elevation. As a result, the building is naturally insulated.

The winery began life as sparkling wines exclusively. In 1999, facility opened, it was rechristened the Spanish Catalan language of the Raventos also own Codorniu in 450 years of winemaking experience Codorniu Napa, which produced eight years after the $30 million Artesa, which means "craftsman" in owners, the Raventos family. The Catalonia, where the family boasts and a 125-year history as one of Europe's leading producers of sparkling wine made in the traditional *méthode champenoise*. Rather than fermented in a barrel, the wine is fermented in the bottle from which it will be poured. The transformation into a facility that also specializes in still wines took three years and $10 million.

The winery interior has a peaceful courtyard with sculptures, a fountain, and a pool of water. The tasting room with its curved wooden bar has a picture-window view of the courtyard. Artesa's commitment to fine arts is revealed in its extensive collection, including a large bronze by Spanish sculptor Marcel Marti in front of a reflecting pool. Gordon Huether exhibits works in various media, particularly glass and metal, throughout the visitor center. Among the newer features are a museum and the Carneros Center, which educates visitors about the human history, natural history, topography, and scenic beauty of the appellation. The museum displays antique winemaking equipment, including sixteenth-century Spanish wine casks and Greek wine cups from 400 B.C.

Looking closely at the Artesa label, one sees elements of the winery's architecture, its sculpture, and its prismlike windows, as well as a triangle, a shape representing balance that is repeated often throughout the property. The label's use of gold signifies, of course, excellence.

BEAULIEU VINEYARDS

BEAULIEU VINEYARDS
1960 Hwy. 29
Rutherford, CA 94573
707-967-5233
bv.feedback@guinnessudv.
com
www.BVwine.com

OWNER: Diageo Chateau & Estates Wines.

LOCATION: About 3 miles south of St. Helena.

APPELLATION: Napa Valley.

HOURS: 10 A.M.–5 P.M. daily.

TASTINGS: $5 for 4 wines in main tasting room; $25 for 5 wines in Georges de Latour Reserve Room.

TOURS: Hourly, 11 A.M.–4 P.M. Mon.–Fri.; 11 A.M., 12 noon, 1 P.M., and thereafter on half hour until 4 P.M. Sat.–Sun.

THE WINES: Cabernet Sauvignon, Chardonnay, Merlot, Muscat, Pinot Gris, Pinot Noir, Sangiovese, Sparkling Wine (Brut), Syrah, vintage Port, Viognier, Zinfandel.

SPECIALTY: Georges de Latour Private Reserve Cabernet Sauvignon.

WINEMAKERS: Joel Aiken, Robert Masyzcek, and Jeffrey Stambor.

ANNUAL PRODUCTION: 1.3 million cases.

OF SPECIAL NOTE: Tastings of Signet Series, a line of limited production wines, on first weekend of each month ($5). BV label *tapenade* and other condiments, wine, cookbooks, and Spa Napa Valley products available in gift shop.

NEARBY ATTRACTIONS: Bothe-Napa State Park (hiking, picnicking, horseback riding, swimming Memorial Day–Labor Day); Bale Grist Mill State Historic Park (water-powered mill circa 1846); Silverado Museum (Robert Louis Stevenson memorabilia).

In the winter of 2001, Beaulieu Vineyards commissioned a bronze sculpture of its late, legendary winemaker, André Tchelistcheff. The life-size statue depicting the "Maestro" at his craft, created by noted sculptor William Behrends (who rendered Willie Mays for the San Francisco Giants ballpark), was unveiled at a gala at the Culinary Institute of America at Greystone, where it will remain until late 2003, when it will move to its permanent home at the winery.

For all the fanfare, it is a relatively modest tribute to Tchelistcheff, an acclaimed innovator and mentor to many winemakers, including current BV winemaker Joel Aiken. Tchelistcheff came to the winery in 1938 from the Pasteur Institute in Paris. As its master enologist for thirty-five years and as a consultant in the early 1990s, he developed techniques and technologies still used by the winery today. The first vintage of BV Private Reserve Cabernet Sauvignon, widely acknowledged for setting the standard for reserve-style Napa Cabernets in the 1930s, was the signature creation of the Russian-born master, who died in 1994 at the age of ninety-two.

The brilliant man who hired Tchelistcheff was Georges de Latour, the Frenchman who established the winery in 1900 on four acres in Rutherford. He named it Beaulieu, meaning "beautiful place" in French, and immediately began expanding his holdings. When Napa vineyards began to be destroyed by the tiny *Phylloxera* louse, de Latour imported louse-resistant vines from Europe to plant on his estate vineyards. When Prohibition threatened the entire industry, de Latour kept his business going by supplying altar wine to the Catholic Church. At the end of Prohibition, he picked the Russian winemaker to resuscitate full-scale production.

Tchelistcheff confirmed de Latour's wise instincts by producing a series of award-winning Cabernets that put the winery on the firm footing it would need when the founder died in 1940. The winemaker continued to work with Fernande de Latour, de Latour's widow—who renamed the reserve Cabernet Sauvignon in honor of her husband—and later with her daughter, Helene de Pins.

With its ivy-clad stone buildings and red-tile roofs, Beaulieu Vineyards is one of the prettiest wineries in Napa. The older structures are the work of Hamdon McIntire, who also designed Inglenook, Greystone, and Far Niente. Adjacent to the winemaking facilities is a small, wisteria-shaded building where Georges de Latour Private Reserve Cabernet Sauvignon is sampled. The main tasting room lies beyond, in an interesting octagonal structure that houses the tasting bar on the main level and a gift shop at the bottom of a spiral staircase.

BERINGER VINEYARDS

With the 1883 Rhine House, hand-carved aging tunnels, and a heritage dating to 1876, Beringer Vineyards is steeped in history like few other wineries in California. The oldest continuously operating winery in the Napa Valley, it combines age-old traditions with up-to-date technology to create a wide range of award-winning wines.

It was German know-how that set the Beringer brothers on the path to glory. Jacob and Frederick Beringer emigrated from Mainz, Germany, to the United States in the 1860s. Jacob, having worked in cellars in Germany, was intrigued when he heard that the California climate was ideal for growing the varietal grapes that flourished in Europe's winemaking regions. Leaving Frederick in New York, he traveled west in 1870 to discover that the Napa Valley's rocky, well-drained soils were similar to those in his native Rhine  Valley. Five years later, he bought land with Frederick and began excavating the hillsides to create tunnels for aging his wines. The brothers founded Beringer Vineyards in 1876. During the building of the caves and winery, Jacob lived in an 1848 farmhouse now known as Hudson House. The meticulously restored and expanded structure now serves as Beringer Vineyards' Culinary Arts Center.

But the star attraction on the lavishly landscaped grounds is unquestionably the seventeen-room Rhine House, which Frederick modeled after his ancestral home in Germany. The redwood, brick, and stucco mansion is painted in the original Tudor color scheme of earth tones, and the original slate still covers the gabled roof and exterior. The interior is graced with myriad gems of craftsmanship such as Belgian art nouveau–style stained-glass windows.

The winery's standard tour encompasses a visit to the cellars and the hand-dug aging tunnels in the Old Stone Winery, where tasting is available. Beringer also offers programs that provide visitors more in-depth experiences. The Vintage Legacy Tour focuses on the winery's history. Blush Wine-and-Food-in-Balance includes a wine-and-food-pairing demonstration. Picnic at Beringer starts at the original St. Helena Home Vineyard and proceeds through the Old Stone Winery prior to a three-course alfresco lunch in the Redwood Grove, prepared by Beringer Vineyards executive chef David Frakes.

BERINGER VINEYARDS
2000 Main St.
St. Helena, CA 94574
707-963-7115
www.beringer.com

OWNER: Beringer Blass Wine Estates.

LOCATION: On Hwy. 29 about .5 mile north of St. Helena.

APPELLATION: Napa Valley.

HOURS: 10 A.M.–5 P.M. daily in winter, 10 A.M.–6 P.M. daily in summer.

TASTINGS: 3 wines with tour fee; à la carte fees for Reserve Tasting Room; $5 for 3 nonreserve wines in Old Stone Winery.

TOURS: 45-minute tours ($5) every half hour, 10:30 A.M.–4 P.M. Vintage Legacy Tour ($30), Blush Wine-and-Food-in-Balance ($10), and Picnic at Beringer ($65) by reservation.

THE WINES: Cabernet Franc, Cabernet Sauvignon, Cabernet Sauvignon Port, Chardonnay, Chenin Blanc, Gamay Beaujolais, Gewürztraminer, Johannisberg Riesling, Merlot, Pinot Noir, Sauvignon Blanc, Shiraz, White Merlot, White Zinfandel.

SPECIALTIES: Private Reserve Chardonnay, Cabernet Sauvignon.

WINEMAKERS: Ed Sbragia, wine master; Laurie Hook, winemaker.

ANNUAL PRODUCTION: Unavailable.

OF SPECIAL NOTE: Tour includes visit to barrel storage caves hand-chiseled by Chinese laborers in late 1800s.

NEARBY ATTRACTIONS: Bothe-Napa State Park (hiking, picnicking, horseback riding, swimming Memorial Day–Labor Day); Bale Grist Mill State Historic Park (water-powered mill circa 1846); Silverado Museum (Robert Louis Stevenson memorabilia).

CAKEBREAD CELLARS

CAKEBREAD CELLARS
8300 Hwy. 29
Rutherford, CA 94573
707-963-5222
800-588-0298
cellars@cakebread.com
www.cakebread.com

OWNERS: Cakebread family.

LOCATION: Between
Oakville and Rutherford
on Hwy. 29.

APPELLATION: Napa Valley.

HOURS: 10 A.M.–4 P.M. daily.

TASTINGS: Cellars Tasting,
$5 for 3 wines; Vintners
Tasting, $10 for 5 wines.

TOURS: 75-minute tour
and guided tasting at
10:30 A.M. and 2 P.M. daily,
by reservation.

THE WINES: Cabernet
Sauvignon, Chardonnay,
Merlot, Pinot Noir,
Rubaiyat, Sauvignon
Blanc, Syrah.

SPECIALTIES: Benchlands
Select and Three Sisters
Cabernet Sauvignon,
Rubaiyat.

WINEMAKER:
Julianne Laks.

ANNUAL PRODUCTION:
Under 85,000 cases.

OF SPECIAL NOTE:
Occasional cooking classes
led by winery chefs.
Annual American Harvest
Workshop held in
September, with some
lectures on food and wine
open to public. Pinot
Noir, Syrah, Rubaiyat,
and Vinehill Cabernet
Sauvignon available only
at winery. Estate-grown
produce sold from early
summer through harvest.

NEARBY ATTRACTIONS:
Napa Valley Museum
(winemaking displays, art
exhibits); Silverado
Museum (Robert Louis
Stevenson memorabilia).

There's no giant sign on the highway announcing this winery, just a mailbox with the name. Regardless of the time of year, plants are in bloom along the driveway leading to the small parking lot and barnlike building complex. There's an intimacy to the modest setting that suggests this is a family concern. The Cakebreads have built their business into one of the best-known Napa wineries producing fewer than 85,000 cases.

Not only is Cakebread family owned, but it is truly family operated. Jack and Dolores Cakebread and their three sons and daughters-in-law have all been instrumental in guiding the winery to success over the past three decades.

It all started when Jack and Dolores were in high school. They worked well together from the beginning, helping Jack's parents at their Contra Costa County ranch during the peach and almond harvests. The sweethearts married in 1950, and Jack took over his father's car repair business in Oakland. But this was not to be his ultimate career. Jack was also a photographer who had studied with Ansel Adams and in 1972 was given the job of photographing the wine country for the *Treasury of American Wines*.

In the course of this new assignment, he looked up old friends at the Sturdivant Ranch and mentioned he was interested in acquiring vineyard property. The Sturdivants were ready to sell to Jack and Dolores, who promptly christened the place Cakebread Cellars. For years, they continued their business in Oakland, closing up shop on Friday afternoons and taking their young sons up to the Napa ranch for the weekends. While Jack, Steve, Bruce, and Dennis worked in the vineyards, Dolores began the vegetable and flower gardens that would become an integral part of the winery's extensive hospitality program.

Bruce grew up to study viticulture and enology at the University of California at Davis, which prepared him to become winemaker in time for the 1978 harvest. Dennis took the business route and since 1986 has managed sales and marketing. Karen, married to eldest son Steve, assists Dolores with hospitality events and produces the popular American Harvest Workshop each fall. After serving as enologist for twelve years, Julianne Laks became the winemaker in 2002.

Cakebread Cellars is surrounded by a lush garden with a fountain wall and a pond shared by fish, ducks, and geese. A barbecue area for cooking and dining alfresco is set beneath valley oaks and weeping willows. The winery's two chefs have their pick of fresh vegetables, herbs, and edible flowers, as do the amateur cooks who flock to Cakebread's cooking classes. Any extra produce is available for purchase at the winery's summertime produce stand.

Cakebread Cellars

NAPA VALLEY
Chardonnay
2000

ALCOHOL 14.1% BY VOLUME

CHIMNEY ROCK WINERY

Shaded by a grove of poplar trees, Chimney Rock's pristine white Cape Dutch buildings, with their steep, slate-gray roofs and curving, arched gables, complement their pastoral setting. The distinctive architecture was inspired by the many years that the winery's founders spent in South Africa. The late Sheldon "Hack" Wilson and his wife, Stella, had worked abroad for decades in the soft drink, brewing, restaurant, and luxury hotel businesses, developing a taste for fine wine along the way. Not surprisingly, they began their search for winery property in France. When a couple of potential sites in Bordeaux failed to materialize, they turned their attention to California and found what they were looking for in the Napa Valley.

Wilson's research convinced him that the soils and microclimates of the Stags Leap District would produce the quality of grapes for the style of wine he had in mind. When he saw the rustic Chimney Rock Golf Course, he could easily envision rows of grapevines in place of fairways. In 1980, the Wilsons purchased the golf course as well as the adjacent mountain, bulldozed nine of the eighteen holes, and planted vineyards on seventy-five acres. The first vintage was produced in 1984, and the winery's production building was completed five years later.

Douglas Fletcher was already an old hand at Stags Leap winemaking when he came on board in 1987, having worked at nearby Steltzner Vineyards. He was joined recently by assistant winemaker Elizabeth Vianna, a Brazilian-born enologist who had worked at Chimney Rock as an intern in 1999. Together, they focus on handcrafting wines mostly from Bordeaux varietals.

In 2000, the remaining fairways at Chimney Rock were converted to sixty-three acres of Cabernet Sauvignon vineyards. All of the winery's red-wine vineyards are in the Stags Leap District. The colorful name of this part of southern Napa stems from the legend of an agile buck seen bounding along a jagged outcropping of rock to elude hunters. The appellation extends south along the Silverado Trail from the Yountville Cross Road for three miles, bordered on the east by craggy hillsides and on the west by the Napa River.

Picturesque at any time of year, Chimney Rock Winery is especially appealing in spring and summer, when aromatic mauve Angel Face roses climb the columns in front of the hospitality center. The tasting room has white walls and dark exposed beams. On the far side, doors open onto a courtyard set with tables, chairs, and white market umbrellas and planted with a bevy of rosebushes bearing ivory flowers.

CHIMNEY ROCK WINERY
5350 Silverado Trail
Napa, CA 94558
707-257-2641
www.chimneyrock.com

OWNERS: Terlato Wine Group and Wilson family.

LOCATION: 3 miles south of Yountville.

APPELLATION: Stag's Leap District.

HOURS: 10 A.M.–5 P.M. daily.

TASTINGS: $7 for 4 wines.

TOURS: Group tours by appointment only.

THE WINES: Cabernet Franc, Cabernet Sauvignon, Elevage (red Meritage).

SPECIALTY: Cabernet Sauvignon.

WINEMAKER: Douglas Fletcher.

ANNUAL PRODUCTION: 18,000 cases.

OF SPECIAL NOTE: Some limited-production wines available only in tasting room.

NEARBY ATTRACTIONS: Napa Valley Museum (winemaking displays, art exhibits).

DOMAINE CARNEROS

DOMAINE CARNEROS
1240 Duhig Rd.
Napa, CA 94559
707-257-0101
info@domainecarneros.com
www.domainecarneros.com

OWNERS: Champagne
Taittinger and Kobrand
Corporation.

LOCATION: Intersection of
Hwys. 121/12 and Duhig
Rd., 4 miles southwest
of town of Napa.

APPELLATION: Carneros.

HOURS: 10 A.M.–6 P.M. daily.

TASTINGS: $5.50–$10 per
glass, depending on
variety; $13.50 for sampler
of 3 sparkling wines,
Monday–Thursday. All
wines served with hors
d'oeuvres.

TOURS: Hourly, 11 A.M.–
4 P.M. Group tours for
10 or more by appoint-
ment include glass of
Domaine Carneros wine
and hors d'oeuvres.

THE WINES: Pinot Noir,
sparkling wine.

SPECIALTIES: *Méthode
champenoise* sparkling
wine, Pinot Noir.

WINEMAKER: Eileen Crane.

ANNUAL PRODUCTION:
45,000 cases.

OF SPECIAL NOTE: Table
service available on terrace
with panoramic views of
Carneros region. Cheese
plates and caviar available
for purchase. Books on
wine and food sold in
winery shop.

NEARBY ATTRACTION:
di Rosa Preserve (indoor
and outdoor exhibits of
works by contemporary
Bay Area artists).

An architectural tribute to its French heritage, the chateau that houses Domaine Carneros would look at home in Champagne, France. It dominates a hillside in the renowned Carneros region in southern Napa, prime growing area for the grape varieties that go into the best sparkling wine and sumptuous Pinot Noir. The opulent winery is approached by a long series of steps that climb to a grand entranceway. French marble floors, high ceilings, and decorative features such as a Louis XV fireplace mantel imbue the interior with a palatial ambience. Guests are welcome to order wines in the elegant salon, warmed by a fireplace on cool days, or on the terrace.

Established in 1987, Domaine Carneros is a joint venture between Champagne Taittinger of France and Kobrand Corporation. President Director-General Claude Taittinger led the extensive search for the ideal site for making world-class sparkling wine. The Carneros region's long, moderately cool growing season the summer heat allow for perfect acidic balance in donnay grapes. Domaine yards totaling 200 acres in

and the fog that mitigates slow, even ripening and the Pinot Noir and Char- Carneros farms three vine- the appellation.

Harvest at Domaine August, when workers head Carneros begins in mid- out to pick grapes before dawn. A delicate balance of sugar and acidity is required for the best sparkling wine. The fruit is immediately brought to the press for the gentle extracting of the juice. From that moment through vinification, each lot is maintained separately before the exact blend is determined. The sparkling wines are made in accordance with the traditional *méthode champenoise,* in which secondary fermentation takes place in the bottle, not the tank. The grapes for Pinot Noir are gathered a week or two after the sparkling wine harvest is complete, then are fermented for ten days. After this, the juices are siphoned off, and the fruit is gently pressed to extract the remaining juice. The resulting wine is aged in French oak barrels for up to ten months before bottling.

In charge of these elaborate procedures is Managing Director Eileen Crane, who worked at Domaine Chandon and later served as winemaker and vice president of nearby Gloria Ferrer Champagne Caves. This experience—combined with the vision she shares with Taittinger on how to produce the elegant and delicate, yet intense sparkling wines—made her the ideal choice for overseeing the planning and development of Domaine Carneros. Crane focuses on making the most of the winery's fortuitous combination of climate, California technology, and French expertise to create wines of great character.

DUCKHORN VINEYARDS

Even if you were led blindfolded into this winery, you would have a good chance of guessing its name. One clue is the large mural of a duck-filled marsh on the wall in the tasting room. Another is a collection of duck prints. Still stumped? Take a look at the numerous cases filled with antique hunting decoys in the form of blue wing teal, mallards, and pintails, all displayed neatly on glass shelves.

Dan Duckhorn is actually a duck fancier, as coincidence would have it. Despite these decorative details, the emphasis is squarely on his winery's three Bordeaux varietals, the most notable of which is Merlot. Dan and Margaret Duckhorn, who had earlier been in the vineyard nursery business, traveled extensively in Pomerol and St. Emilion, the Bordeaux appellations where Merlot is king. They then decided to create their own version.

In 1976, the Duckhorns, along with ten other families, purchased the ten acres in St. Helena where the winery is now located. The first vintage of Duckhorn Merlot, in 1978, came from the esteemed Three Palms Vineyard a few miles up the Silverado Trail. Although Dan and Margaret Duckhorn also started making Cabernet Sauvignon that year and added Sauvignon Blanc in 1982, the winery is most often associated with the Merlots made from its estate vineyards and the Three Palms' grapes.

Over the next twenty-four years, Duckhorn Vineyards expanded its annual production from sixteen hundred cases to sixty-five thousand, but during that time, the winery lacked a bona fide tasting room. Finally, in the fall of 2000, Duckhorn debuted its new facility, a farm-style Victorian with a wraparound porch. Extensively planted with evergreen trees and shrubs, the surrounding gardens have a Mediterranean look, with lots of lavender and native grasses. There are so many fountains that visitors can hear gurgling water from virtually any of the wooden benches arranged throughout the property. Colorful camellias in winter and rhododendrons in early spring are followed by blooming roses and purple butterfly bushes that attract a plethora of beneficial insects. Comfortable rattan sofas and chairs beckon from the front porch.

Inside the contemporary tasting room, casement windows on three sides allow for cross breezes and views of the vineyards and the forested hills to the west. Visitors are comfortably seated and served at a variety of marble-topped tables set with mats, glasses, tasting notes, and even a spit bucket. They are also treated to a bird's-eye look at the mural of one of Dan Duckhorn's favorite duck-hunting haunts at the base of the Sutter Buttes.

DUCKHORN VINEYARDS
1000 Lodi Ln.
St. Helena, CA 94574
707-963-7108
welcome@duckhorn.com
www.duckhorn.com

OWNER: Duckhorn
Wine Company.

LOCATION: 3 miles north
of St. Helena at Silverado
Trail.

APPELLATION: Napa Valley.

HOURS: 10 A.M.–4 P.M. daily.

TASTINGS: Walk-in and by
appointment.

TOURS: By appointment.

THE WINES: Cabernet
Sauvignon, Merlot,
Sauvignon Blanc.

SPECIALTIES: Estate-grown
and vineyard-designated
wines.

WINEMAKER:
Mark Beringer.

ANNUAL PRODUCTION:
65,000 cases.

OF SPECIAL NOTE: Bottle
limits on some wines.
Annual events include
Spring Open House (May).

NEARBY ATTRACTIONS:
Bothe-Napa State Park
(hiking, picnicking, horse-
back riding, swimming
Memorial Day–Labor
Day); Bale Grist Mill State
Historic Park (water-
powered mill circa 1846);
Silverado Museum
(Robert Louis Stevenson
memorabilia).

EDGEWOOD ESTATE WINERY

EDGEWOOD ESTATE WINERY
401 Hwy. 29
St. Helena, CA 94574
707-963-7293
www.edgewoodestate.com

OWNER: Golden State
Vintners.

LOCATION: About 1.5 miles
south of downtown
St. Helena.

APPELLATION: Napa Valley.

HOURS: 10 A.M.–5:30 P.M.
daily.

TASTINGS: $5 for 5 wines.

TOURS: None.

THE WINES: Cabernet
Franc, Cabernet
Sauvignon, Chardonnay,
Malbec, Merlot, Petite
Sirah, Petit Verdot, Pinot
Noir, Port, Zinfandel.

SPECIALTIES: Classic red
Bordeaux varietals.

WINEMAKER: Jeff Gaffner.

ANNUAL PRODUCTION:
11,000 cases.

OF SPECIAL NOTE: Picnic
area on trellised patio with
vineyard and mountain
views.

NEARBY ATTRACTIONS:
Silverado Museum
(Robert Louis Stevenson
memorabilia).

In the spring of 2002, this historic winery hosted an amazing event: a vertical tasting of its Malbecs from 1992 to 2001. The 2000 and the 2001 were still in barrels, but it is doubtful that any other California winery could boast ten vintages of a lesser-known Bordeaux varietal. Edgewood Estate Winery has clearly distinguished itself not only with Malbec, but as one of the few Napa Valley wineries that produces the full complement of classic red Bordeaux varietals. Like that French appellation—which literally means "close to the water"—Napa Valley's proximity to the sea provides the consistently moderate climate considered ideal for growing these premium grapes.

Although Edgewood Estate Winery was technically founded in 1994, its roots run deep in the Napa soil. There's actually a winery within a winery at this historic property. Inside the rambling winemaking facility, in plain sight, is the original structure, built in 1885 by New England sea captain William Peterson. It  was enveloped by the much larger building constructed a half century later.

Peterson sold his forty-acre namesake winery in 1891 to Robert Bergfeld, who developed it under his own name. Unfortunately, after the 1906 earthquake, he went out of business. The winery was resurrected in 1910 by Theodore Gier, who expanded it to serve as headquarters of a wine-making operation that extended to Livermore in the East Bay. In 1935, a collection of innovative grape growers, the Napa Valley Cooperative, bought the estate. For the next sixty years, the group revamped the facilities and brought back the Bergfeld name. The landmark property changed hands again in 1994, when it was purchased by the O'Neill family of Golden State Vintners and reopened as Edgewood Estate Winery. In 1999, the tasting room from the 1980s was remodeled, giving it redwood walls and sliding glass doors that afford views of the Mayacamas and Vaca Ranges.

The estate vineyard consists of thirty acres of classic Bordeaux varieties. Edgewood has also established long-term relationships with other grape growers, whose vineyard lots are kept separate throughout the winemaking process. As a result, the winery can track, analyze, and refine viticultural procedures at all their source vineyards.

The winemaking is in the hands of Jeff Gaffner, a second-generation grape grower from Sonoma County whose twenty years' experience includes posts at Chateau St. Jean and Benziger Family Winery. A self-declared traditionalist, Gaffner appreciates the winery's focus on the classics: "The greatest thing about working with all of the Bordeaux varietals is the opportunity to cook with more than one spice. Each of these varieties brings its own distinctive character to the wine."

FLORA SPRINGS WINERY AND VINEYARDS

This winery's history is a cautionary tale of sorts: Be careful what you wish for. In 1977, Jerry and Flora Komes were looking for a place to relax and watch the grapes grow. Their search led them to the Napa Valley, which has countless porches with vineyard views. Even then, they weren't thinking of growing the grapes themselves, let alone making wine.

Then the couple saw the 1956 Louis M. Martini house in the western foothills. Louis had died three years previously, and the property was looking rather shabby. Two of the buildings, the 1888 Rennie Winery and the 1885 Charles Brockhoff Winery, were filled with bats, rats, and rattlesnakes. The place looked more like a ghost town than a potential residence, but it had the key ingredient: the very views that the Komeses desired. As Jerry Komes recalled, "Outside of a home, it had all the things we weren't looking for."

The couple bought the package and, inspired by the legacy of the land, decided to restore the property. Like so many other retirement projects, this one became a consuming passion that threatened the prospect of leisurely afternoons rocking on the porch. Before long, the property served as a magnet, luring two of Jerry and Flora's children. Son John, a general contractor and home winemaker, was fascinated by the challenges of producing wine and breathing life into the aged buildings. Daughter Julie and her husband, Pat Garvey, gave up careers in education, and Pat dedicated himself to learning the grape-growing business.

Another son, Mike, also become a partner. After two vintages, John decided that he and Julie had pressed their luck as winemakers to the limit, and Ken Deis was hired. More than two decades later, he's still at it.

John's wife, Carrie, gets the credit for naming the new winery. There were two obvious life-giving sources to this venture, Flora herself and the continuously flowing springs that were the sole source of water for the property. Flora Springs had almost immediate success. The first commercially released wine, a Chardonnay, won a gold medal at the prestigious Los Angeles County Fair, the beginning of many awards for the winery.

Over the years, the family has acquired six hundred acres of vineyards in nine distinct Napa Valley locations, in addition to the original Komes Ranch. The winery sells 80 percent of these grapes to twenty-five premium wineries, which gives Flora Springs a unique opportunity to select the 20 percent that fits the winery's criteria. Visitors sample Flora Springs wines about a mile north of the actual winery at the tasting room, which has a newly refurbished rooftop deck.

FLORA SPRINGS WINERY AND VINEYARDS
677 Hwy. 29
St. Helena, CA 94574
707-967-8032
fswinery@aol.com
www.florasprings.com

OWNERS: Komes/Garvey families.

LOCATION: About 1.5 miles south of downtown St. Helena.

APPELLATION: Napa Valley.

HOURS: Tasting room: 10 A.M.–5 P.M. daily.

TASTINGS: $5 for 6 wines; $8 for 5 or 6 reserve wines.

TOURS: Of winery by appointment on Friday afternoons.

THE WINES: Cabernet Sauvignon, Chardonnay, Merlot, Pinot Grigio, Pinot Noir, Sangiovese, Sauvignon Blanc, Trilogy (Meritage blend).

SPECIALTY: Trilogy.

WINEMAKER: Ken Deis.

ANNUAL PRODUCTION: 50,000 cases.

OF SPECIAL NOTE: Winery tour includes newly completed caves.

NEARBY ATTRACTIONS: Bothe-Napa State Park (hiking, picnicking, horseback riding, swimming Memorial Day–Labor Day); Bale Grist Mill State Historic Park (water-powered mill circa 1846); Silverado Museum (Robert Louis Stevenson memorabilia).

FRANCISCAN OAKVILLE ESTATE

FRANCISCAN OAKVILLE ESTATE
1178 Galleron Rd.
St. Helena, CA 94574
707-963-7111
800-529-WINE (9463)
winemaker@franciscan.com
www.franciscan.com

OWNER: Franciscan Estates, Fine Wine Division of Constellation Brands.

LOCATION: Off Hwy. 29 just north of Rutherford.

APPELLATION: Napa Valley.

HOURS: 10 A.M.–5 P.M. daily.

TASTINGS: $5 for 4 wines; $10 for 4 reserve wines.

TOURS: None.

THE WINES: Cabernet Sauvignon, Chardonnay, Cuvée Sauvage (wild yeast–fermented Chardonnay), Magnificat (red Meritage blend), Merlot, Zinfandel.

SPECIALTIES: Cuvée Sauvage, Magnificat.

WINEMAKER: Larry Levin.

ANNUAL PRODUCTION: 170,000 cases.

OF SPECIAL NOTE: Taste Exploration series ($10) allows up to 8 visitors to explore wine from vineyard to bottle. Topics include blending, appellations, and Pinot Noir clones. Sessions last 30–45 minutes and are offered daily at 11 A.M. and 2 P.M. Riedel Tastings held hourly, 11 A.M.–3 P.M.

NEARBY ATTRACTIONS: Bothe-Napa State Park (hiking, picnicking, horseback riding, swimming Memorial Day–Labor Day); Bale Grist Mill State Historic Park (waterpowered mill circa 1846); Silverado Museum (Robert Louis Stevenson memorabilia).

The elegant courtyard fountain at the entrance to the hospitality center, with its curves and scalloped edges, welcomes visitors with restrained exuberance. Polished wooden benches, strategically placed around the landscaped grounds, silently urge everyone to take a break and soak it all in. When guests enter the modern ocher-and-mustard-colored building, which opened in 2001, they are glad to sit down for a minute.

Once inside, visitors have some decisions to make because the tastings at Franciscan Oakville Estate follow several formats. Depending on guests' interests and the day's offerings, options range from four current releases or reserve wines in the tasting room, to in-depth guided tastings that may focus on reserve wines or blending, to a short course that involves sampling various wines in different Riedel glasses. Personalized sessions may also be arranged in advance. All of the special tastings are held in private rooms.

Many wine enthusiasts are content to linger in the handsome tasting room, lit from above by daylight flooding in from a full-length clerestory. Dark wood display cases holding a good selection of coffee-table books and handpainted pottery contrast with sand-colored walls and a stone floor. The four-sided walnut bar is ringed with a zinc countertop. To the left of the entry, double doors open onto a garden courtyard. The south end of the building houses a luxurious lounge for wine club members and the wine library, where more than twenty-five years of Franciscan's history in the Napa Valley are on display—in bottles.

That history dates to 1972, the year Raymond Duncan and the late Justin Meyer (winemaking partners who also owned Silver Oak Cellars) founded the winery. In 1978, the Peter Eckes Company of Germany purchased the Franciscan brand and most of the estate vineyards, some three hundred acres in Napa's Oakville District and an equal amount in Sonoma County's Alexander Valley. Duncan and Meyer held on to a parcel of the original property for Silver Oak. Justin Meyer stayed on as president of Franciscan, but not for long, as Silver Oak beckoned. The Eckes Company found a new president in Agustin Huneeus, a Chilean who had built the Concha y Toro winery in his native country. Huneeus steered Franciscan back on track by using estate grapes instead of buying lesser-quality fruit from other sources and selling off the Franciscan grapes. In 1986, recognizing the distinctions between the Napa Valley and the Sonoma County vineyards, he created a separate brand, Estancia, for the Alexander Valley estate. Reflecting that the home winery's fruit comes from its vineyards in Napa Valley's Oakville District, the name was formally changed to Franciscan Oakville Estate.

FREEMARK ABBEY WINERY

FREEMARK ABBEY WINERY
3022 St. Helena Hwy.
North
St. Helena, CA 94574
800-963-9698
wineinfo@freemarkabbey.com
www.freemarkabbey.com

OWNER: Legacy Estates Group.

LOCATION: 2 miles north of St. Helena at Lodi Ln.

APPELLATION: Napa Valley.

HOURS: 10 A.M.–5 P.M. daily, October–May; until 6 P.M. June–September.

TASTINGS: $5 for 5 wines.

TOURS: By appointment.

THE WINES: Cabernet Franc, Cabernet Sauvignon, Chardonnay, Edelwein Gold (late-harvest Riesling), Merlot, Petite Sirah, Riesling, Sangiovese, Viognier.

SPECIALTIES: Sycamore Vineyards, Bosché Vineyards, and Napa Valley Cabernet Sauvignons; Edelwein Gold.

WINEMAKERS: Ted Edwards, director of winemaking, and Tim Bell.

ANNUAL PRODUCTION: 45,000 cases.

OF SPECIAL NOTE: Visitors are welcome to picnic at tables set on lawn. Cabernet Franc, Petite Sirah, and Sangiovese available only at winery.

NEARBY ATTRACTIONS: Bothe-Napa State Park (hiking, picnicking, horseback riding, swimming Memorial Day–Labor Day); Bale Grist Mill State Historic Park (water-powered mill circa 1846); Silverado Museum (Robert Louis Stevenson memorabilia).

Of the many reasons people move to the Napa Valley and start a winery, the founder of Freemark Abbey may have had the most unlikely. Josephine Marlin Tychson, a native San Lorenzo, California, and her husband, John Tychson, a Danish immigrant, moved to St. Helena in 1881 in hopes that the region's climate would ameliorate John's tuberculosis. The couple, who had long wanted to make wine from their own vineyards, purchased acreage north of St. Helena for $8,500. They built their home on what later became known as Tychson Hill.

Using only a horse and plow, they began to expand their holdings by adding some ten acres of vines each year. John died in 1886, leaving Josephine to oversee the construction of a small winery that crushed 110 tons in 1890, producing Zinfandel, Riesling, and a Burgundy-style blend. Josephine Tychson was the first woman to build 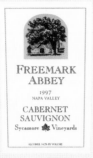 and operate a winery in California.

When an outbreak of the root louse *Phylloxera* began affecting her vineyards in 1893, Josephine sold the winery and some of her vineyards. The winery changed hands over the years, but the original wooden building survived until 1906, when it was replaced with one made of hand-cut stone from nearby Glass Mountain. In 1939, following Prohibition, three Southern Californians—Charles Freeman, Markquand Foster, and Albert "Abbey" Ahern—purchased the property and reopened the winery, combining parts of their names to come up with Freemark Abbey.

After a succession of other owners, a group of seven partners took over and resurrected the winery in 1967. Today, Freemark Abbey is making Riesling, as it did more than a century ago, but it is better known for its Cabernet Sauvignons and Chardonnays. The Cabernets from the Bosché and Sycamore vineyards were among the first wines in California to be named after specific vineyards. Another signature wine is the Edelwein Gold, a late-harvest Riesling. The tasting room is at the far end of a suspended walkway tucked into the back of a parking area conveniently located between a restaurant and a brew pub. The ideal place to savor wine is on a stone patio behind the tasting room, in the shade of market umbrellas.

GRGICH HILLS CELLAR

GRGICH HILLS CELLAR
1829 St. Helena Hwy.
Rutherford, CA 94573
800-532-3057
info@grgich.com
www.grgich.com

OWNERS: Miljenko "Mike" Grgich and Austin Hills.

LOCATION: About 3 miles south of St. Helena.

APPELLATION: Napa Valley.

HOURS: 9:30 A.M.–4:30 P.M. daily.

TASTINGS: $5 for 4 wines.

TOURS: 11 A.M. and 2 P.M. weekdays; 11 A.M. and 1:30 P.M. weekends; holidays by appointment.

THE WINES: Cabernet Sauvignon, Chardonnay, Fumé Blanc, Merlot, Violetta (late-harvest dessert wine), Zinfandel.

SPECIALTY: Chardonnay.

WINEMAKER: Mike Grgich.

ANNUAL PRODUCTION: 80,000 cases.

OF SPECIAL NOTE: Barrel tastings held 2–4 p.m. on Friday afternoons in summer.

NEARBY ATTRACTIONS: Bothe-Napa State Park (hiking, picnicking, horseback riding, swimming Memorial Day–Labor Day); Bale Grist Mill State Historic Park (water-powered mill circa 1846); Silverado Museum (Robert Louis Stevenson memorabilia).

Few people driving along Highway 29 recognize both of the red, white, and blue flags flying in front of this winery. They certainly know one, the American flag. The other represents Croatia, the native country of winemaker and co-owner Miljenko "Mike" Grgich.

The simple red-roofed, white buildings, with vintage farm equipment displayed in front, may not be as flashy as those of nearby wineries, but as the saying goes, it's what's inside that counts. Once visitors pass beneath the grapevine trellis and into the dimly lit recesses of the tasting room, they forget about exterior appearances. The comfortable, old-world atmosphere at Grgich Hills Cellar is not a gimmick.

The winery was founded by Mike Grgich (pronounced GUR-gitch) and Austin E. Hills on July 4, 1977. Both were already well known. Hills is a member of the Hills Brothers coffee family. Grgich was virtually notorious, especially in attention in 1976, when, at the all-French panel of judges chose Chardonnay over the best of the ing. It was a momentous occasion general and in particular for one of the state's top winemakers.

France. He had drawn worldwide now-famous "Paris Tasting," an his 1973 Chateau Montelena white Burgundies in a blind tast- for the California wine industry in Grgich, already acknowledged as Finally in a position to capitalize on his fame, he quickly found a simpatico partner in Hills, who had a background in business and finance and was the owner of established vineyards. The two men shortly began turning out the intensely flavored Chardonnays that remain the flagship wines of Grgich Hills Cellar.

Grgich, easily recognizable with his trademark black beret, was born in 1923 into a winemaking family on the Dalmatian coast of Croatia. He arrived in California in 1958 and spent his early years at Souverain Winery, Christian Brothers at Greystone, and Beaulieu, where he worked with the late, pioneering winemaker André Tchelistcheff before moving on to Mondavi and Chateau Montelena. Grgich continues to make wine and relies on a younger generation—daughter Violet Grgich, vice president of sales and marketing, and nephew Ivo Jeramaz, vice president of production and vineyard development—to carry on the family tradition. Visitors may well run into family members when taking the exceptionally informative winery tour or while sampling wines in the cool, cellarlike tasting room or outside in the shade of the grapevine trellis.

HEITZ WINE CELLARS

Most travelers interested in sampling Heitz wines will visit the tasting room that opened in the spring of 2002 at the original winery site. Palms, traditional symbols of hospitality, greet visitors turning off the highway toward the native-stone building. The parking area is landscaped with Mexican sage, star jasmine, and long-blooming perennials. Demonstration vineyards have been planted in front of the entry doors. Inside, the mahogany floors, cabinets, and long, low tasting bar make for a sophisticated space. Visitors are welcome to amble out to the rear patio, where they find bench seating in the shade of a pergola. The winery's original vineyards, still in use, are just fifteen feet away.

Joe and Alice Heitz met in California in the 1940s. The couple headed north, and while Alice worked in Sacramento, Joe  pursued degrees in enology at the nearby University of California at Davis. Joe Heitz, widely considered a winemaker's winemaker, honed his craft at a few wineries, notably Beaulieu Vineyards, where he spent seven years as understudy to acclaimed winemaker André Tchelistcheff.

Joe and Alice Heitz purchased their first vineyard and winery in 1961. Before long, they outgrew the eight acres and moved to the present 160-acre residence and ranch on Taplin Road, two miles due east from the current tasting room, at the end of a country lane in what locals call Spring Valley. The original winery became the first tasting room, then was replaced by the structure visitors see today. The Taplin Road property was first developed as a winery and vineyard in the 1880s by the Swiss-Italian family of Anton Rossi. Old oaks, rosebushes, wisteria, shaded benches, a couple of small farmhouses, and a beautiful 1898 stone cellar make parts of the ranch look more like a movie set than a working winery. Today, a second generation—winemaker David Heitz and president Kathleen Heitz Myers—oversees the winery's various Napa Valley ranches, which include 360 acres of vineyards.

The most famous wines Heitz makes come from three prestigious Napa Valley Cabernet vineyards: Bella Oaks Vineyard, Trailside Vineyard, and Martha's Vineyard. Perhaps no other vineyard name in the United States is as widely recognized as Martha's Vineyard in Oakville. Owned by the Tom and Martha May family, the thirty-four-acre property produces Cabernet Sauvignon known for its minty characteristics, rich flavors, and overall balance. Heitz Cellars receives all the grapes from the vineyard. So distinctive is the product that in 1966 Joe Heitz began to bottle it separately from his Heitz Napa Valley Cabernet, starting the widespread trend of vintners acknowledging specific vineyards whether they owned them or not.

HEITZ WINE CELLARS
Tasting Room:
436 St. Helena Hwy. South
St. Helena, CA 94574
707-963-2047
Winery:
500 Taplin Rd.
St. Helena, CA 94574
707-963-3542
www.heitzcellar.com

OWNERS: Heitz family.

LOCATION: 2.5 miles south of St. Helena (tasting room).

APPELLATION: Napa Valley.

HOURS: 11 A.M.–4:30 P.M. daily (tasting room).

TASTINGS: Complimentary.

TOURS: Of winery by appointment.

THE WINES: Cabernet Sauvignon, Chardonnay, Grignolino, Grignolino Rosé, Port, Zinfandel.

SPECIALTIES: Vineyard-designated Cabernet Sauvignons.

WINEMAKERS: David Heitz and Joe Norman.

ANNUAL PRODUCTION: 38,000 cases.

OF SPECIAL NOTE: Only producer of Italian variety of Grignolino in Napa Valley.

NEARBY ATTRACTIONS: Bothe-Napa State Park (hiking, picnicking, horseback riding, swimming Memorial Day–Labor Day); Bale Grist Mill State Historic Park (water-powered mill, circa 1846); Silverado Museum (Robert Louis Stevenson memorabilia).

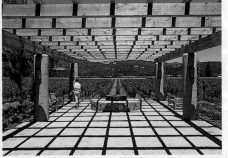

THE HESS COLLECTION WINERY

THE HESS COLLECTION WINERY
4411 Redwood Rd.
Napa, CA 94558
707-255-1144, ext. 237
info@hesscollection.com
www.hesscollection.com

WINERY FOUNDER:
Donald Hess.

LOCATION: About 6 miles
west of Hwy. 29 via
Redwood Rd.

APPELLATION:
Mount Veeder.

HOURS: 10 A.M.–4 P.M. daily.

TASTINGS: $3 for 3 wines.

TOURS: Self-guided tour of
art gallery only.

THE WINES: Cabernet
Sauvignon, Chardonnay,
Merlot, Syrah.

SPECIALTY: Hess Collection
Cabernet Sauvignon.

WINEMAKER: Dave Guffy.

ANNUAL PRODUCTION:
50,000 cases of Hess
Collection.

OF SPECIAL NOTE: Limits
on some bottles; Reserve
and Collection wines
available only in the tasting
room. Slide presentation
on vineyard shown twice
per hour. Children's
section in small wine shop.

NEARBY ATTRACTIONS:
COPIA: The American
Center for Wine, Food
and the Arts.

The Mayacamas Range that defines the western boundary of the Napa Valley, an entirely different landscape than the valley floor, provides unique challenges to the wineries tucked among the peaks and ravines. Shading, cool temperatures, and myriad microclimates make the grapes planted here slower to mature than those in the flatlands, and the poor, rocky soil is constantly threatened by erosion.

Yet when Swiss industrialist Donald Hess decided to found his own winery, he chose Mount Veeder. He based his decision on two broad factors—cool microclimate and excellent soil drainage—that give Mount Veeder grapes the intensity and concentration of aromas and flavors he sought. In 1986, he took over the old Christian Brothers Mont LaSalle winery and began planting Chardonnay and Cabernet Sauvignon and related red varietals. Parts of those vineyards are on ridges so steep that the grapes must be picked by hand. The grapevines, clinging to the steep slopes by extended roots, are so stressed that they tend to produce grapes of exceptional character.

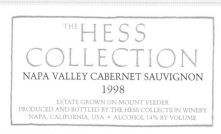

The 285 acres of ninety-five distinctive vineyards, divided into blocks, range in elevation from nine hundred to two thousand feet. The Hess Collection aggressively pursues sustainable farming techniques, which include the use of organic fertilizers, deficit irrigation, cover crops, and mechanical weed control.

Equally impressive is Donald Hess's world-class collection of art by contemporary artists including Francis Bacon, Frank Stella, Robert Rauschenberg, and Robert Motherwell. The 143 works are displayed in huge, well-lit galleries on the second and third floors of the ivy-covered stone building constructed in 1903. Two pieces in particular bring a strong response for their social commentary. One is Argentinian Leopold Maler's *Hommage 1974,* an eternally burning typewriter created in protest of the repression of artistic freedom. The other is Polish sculptor Magdalena Abakanowicz's *Crowd,* a group of nineteen life-size headless figures made of resin and burlap sacks.

The recommended approach is to tour the artworks first, before moving down to the historic first-floor tasting room. Many visitors find they have a lot to talk about while they sip wines from the mountain vineyards, including the room itself. One wall consists of metamorphic sandstone called rhyolite quarried less than a mile from the winery. The stone had been covered with stucco by the Christian Brothers but was inadvertently exposed during the winery's renovation in the late 1980s.

JOSEPH PHELPS VINEYARDS

Joseph Phelps, who built two other wineries before constructing his own in the early 1970s, must have learned a lot about siting large buildings. The imposing redwood structure is invisible from the long, curved driveway until the road crests a knoll and it comes into view. An enormous trellis fashioned from century-old bridge ties and draped with wisteria hangs above the entryway, allowing visitors a glimpse of the vineyards beyond. Small fountains hidden in the ivy emit a constant, refreshing spray in the shade of the trellis.

Joseph Phelps founded his winery in 1972 on what was once a sprawling, 600-acre cattle ranch. Rolling hills, California native oaks, and 160 acres of grapevines characterize the property, located in a corner of the Napa Valley known as Spring Valley. Vistas of this valley, as well as St. Helena and the Mayacamas Range 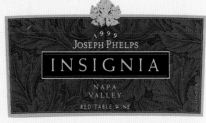 to the west, are plentiful from the rear terrace, which gets plenty of afternoon shade from oak and mimosa trees. Mere yards from the terrace's picnic tables are thriving Cabernet Sauvignon vineyards.

Cabernet Sauvignon has been a major focus since the winery's inception. Joseph Phelps produces three distinct Cabernets under separate labels—Backus Vineyard, Napa Valley, and Insignia, a Bordeaux-style blend. The latter is a blend of the highest quality Cabernet Sauvignon of a particular vintage with other Bordeaux grape varieties from different but complementary sources. With the 1978 release of the 1974 Insignia, the winery became the first in California to produce a blend of traditional Bordeaux grape varieties under a proprietary label. Giving the art of blending a higher priority than both varietal composition and vineyard designation was considered innovative at the time.

Another claim to innovation was Phelps's release of the 1974 Syrah in 1977, a move widely credited with sparking regional interest in the French varietal. Continuing in the same vein, Phelps introduced a new family of Rhone-style wines in 1990, which included Syrah, Viognier, Grenache Rosé, and a red blend called Le Mistral.

Joseph Phelps spent his early years working on his family's farm. He studied engineering and construction management in college and went on to expand his father's Colorado firm into a nationally prominent construction business. One project changed the course of his life. The firm was hired to build Souverain winery (now Rutherford Hill) in Rutherford and then Chateau Souverain in Geyserville. For Phelps, establishing his own winery was the logical next step.

JOSEPH PHELPS VINEYARDS
200 Taplin Rd.
St. Helena, CA 94574
800-707-5789
jpvwines@aol.com
www.jpvwines.com

OWNERS: Principals include Tom Shelton, Craig Williams, Bulmaro Montes, Joseph Phelps, and Damian Parker.

LOCATION: .25 mile east of Silverado Trail between Zinfandel Ln. and Pope St.

APPELLATION: Napa Valley.

HOURS: By appointment; 10 A.M.–5 P.M. Monday–Saturday, 10 A.M.–4 P.M. Sunday.

TASTINGS: $5 for 5 wines; $10 for Insignia.

TOURS: By appointment; 2:30 P.M. Monday–Friday, 10 A.M., 11:30 A.M., 1 P.M., and 2:30 P.M. Saturday and Sunday.

THE WINES: Cabernet Sauvignon, Chardonnay, Eisrebe, Insignia (Bordeaux-style blend), Le Mistral (Rhone-style blend), Merlot, Pastiche (both a red and a white blend), Sauvignon Blanc, Syrah, Viognier.

SPECIALTY: Insignia.

WINEMAKER: Craig Williams.

ANNUAL PRODUCTION: 90,000 cases.

OF SPECIAL NOTE: In-depth technical tastings available at varying prices.

NEARBY ATTRACTIONS: Bothe-Napa State Park (hiking, picnicking, horseback riding, swimming Memorial Day–Labor Day); Bale Grist Mill State Historic Park (water-powered mill circa 1846); Silverado Museum (Robert Louis Stevenson memorabilia).

MARKHAM VINEYARDS

MARKHAM VINEYARDS
2812 St. Helena Hwy.
North
St. Helena, CA 94574
707-963-5292
www.markhamvineyards.com

OWNER:
Mercian Corporation.

LOCATION: 1 mile north of St. Helena on Hwy. 29.

APPELLATION: Napa Valley.

HOURS: 10 A.M.–5 P.M. daily.

TASTINGS: $3 for 4 white wines; $5 for 4 red wines.

TOURS: None.

THE WINES: Cabernet Sauvignon, Chardonnay, Merlot, Petite Sirah, Pinot Noir, Reserve Merlot, Sauvignon Blanc, Zinfandel.

SPECIALTIES: All wines.

WINEMAKER: Kimberlee Jackson Nicholls.

ANNUAL PRODUCTION: 150,000 cases.

OF SPECIAL NOTE: Pinot Noir available only at winery. Craft exhibits, book signings, and art exhibit openings in summer months. Food-and-wine-pairing sessions ($30).

NEARBY ATTRACTIONS: Bothe-Napa State Park (hiking, picnicking, horseback riding, swimming Memorial Day–Labor Day); Bale Grist Mill State Historic Park (water-powered mill circa 1846); Silverado Museum (Robert Louis Stevenson memorabilia).

Few people are surprised to hear that Charles Krug, Schramsberg, and Sutter Home wineries were in business in 1874. Less widely known is that they were the only three wineries operating in the Napa Valley that year, when Jean Laurent founded the St. Helena winery that, less than a century later, would become known as Markham Vineyards.

Laurent, a Frenchman from Bordeaux, arrived in California in 1852, drawn by the lure of the 1849 Gold Rush. When his prospecting failed to pan out, he made his way to the city of Napa in 1868 and began growing vegetables. Laurent quickly assessed the high quality of the soil and, being from Bordeaux, realized the Napa Valley was ideally suited to grapevines. Six years later, he established the Laurent Winery in St. Helena.

After Laurent died in 1890, the property changed hands a number of times. In 1977, it was purchased by Bruce Markham, who had already acquired prime vineyard land on the Napa Valley floor, including 93 acres in Yountville once owned by Inglenook. By 1978, he had added the Calistoga Ranch at the head-lands of the Napa River and the Oak Knoll Vineyard in the Oak Knoll District. Altogether, the Markham estate vineyards now cover 330 acres, including the most recent acquisition, Trubody Vineyards, west of Yountville in the center of the valley. These four areas have distinct microclimates that contribute to the complexity of the wines produced by the winery.

In 1988, the winery and vineyard holdings were sold to Japan's oldest and largest wine company, Mercian Corporation. Despite these changes, many things have remained constant. The current owners have maintained the winery's dedication to producing ultrapremium wines sold at relatively modest prices. The first employee hired by Markham, Bryan Del Bondio, is now president of Markham Vineyards, and Jean Laurent's original stone cellar sits at the heart of the facility.

Stylistically, the winery combines both historic and modern elements, with its old stone and concrete façade, and its subdued red metal roofing supported by round wooden columns. Lily ponds flank the approach to the tasting room, and beyond them, orange and yellow canna lilies provide bursts of color when the plants bloom in spring and summer. The tasting room has an atrium with a large fireplace that warms the huge space on cold days. Displayed throughout are fine art and crafts, from blown-glass torches, to jewelry and Limoges boxes, to hand-decorated ceramic plates, urns, and candlesticks. One side of the room is devoted to changing exhibits by noted artists.

MUMM NAPA VALLEY

For connoisseurs of champagne, relaxing outdoors on a sunny day with a glass of bubbly, good friends, and a vineyard view may be the ultimate pleasure. This is obviously what the founders of Mumm Napa Valley had in mind when they conceived of establishing a winery in North America that could produce a sparkling wine that would live up to Champagne standards.

In 1979, representatives of Champagne Mumm of France and Joseph E. Seagram and Sons of New York began quietly searching for the ideal location. So secretive was their project that they even had a code name for it: Project Lafayette. The point man was the late Guy Devaux, a native of Epernay, the epicenter of France's Champagne district and an expert on *méthode champenoise,* the French style of winemaking in  which the wine undergoes its secondary, bubble-producing fermentation in the very bottle from which it will be drunk. Devaux crisscrossed the United States for four years before settling on Napa Valley, the country's best-known appellation.

The best way to appreciate Mumm Napa Valley is to start with a tour. The winery has a reputation for putting on one of the best in the business, covering the complicated steps necessary to get all those bubbles into each bottle. The best time of year to take the tour is during the harvest season, usually between mid-August and mid-October. However, there is a lot to see at any time of year, and conveniently, the entire tour takes place on one level.

Visitors enter the winery through the wine shop; the tasting veranda is just beyond, with spectacular views of the vineyards and the Mayacamas Range.

Mumm Napa Valley is also noted for its commitment to fine art photography. The winery exhibits the work of many renowned, as well as local, photographers in its expansive galleries. Guests may explore the Photography Galleries at their leisure, even while they enjoy a glass of sparkling wine. Most notable is the private collection of Mathew Adams, grandson of photographer Ansel Adams, on display in the permanent exhibition gallery.

MUMM NAPA VALLEY
8445 Silverado Trail
Rutherford, CA 94573
707-967-7700
mumm_club@
mummcuveenapa.com
www.mummnapavalley.
com

OWNER: Allied Domecq
Wines USA.

LOCATION: East of
Rutherford, 1 mile south
of Rutherford Cross Rd.

APPELLATION: Napa Valley.

HOURS: 10 A.M.–5 P.M. daily.

TASTINGS: 3 half flutes for
$8 and up; $8–12 for
reserve wines.

TOURS: Hourly, 10 A.M.–
3 P.M.

THE WINES: Blanc de
Blancs, Blanc de Noirs,
Brut Prestige, Demi Sec,
DVX, Extra Dry, Sparkling
Pinot Noir, Vintage
Reserve.

SPECIALTY: Sparkling wine
made in traditional French
style.

WINEMAKERS:
Robert McNeill and
Ludovic Dervin.

ANNUAL PRODUCTION:
200,000 cases.

OF SPECIAL NOTE: Demi Sec,
Vintage Reserve, Extra
Dry, Sparkling Pinot Noir,
and magnums available
only at winery.

NEARBY ATTRACTIONS:
Napa Valley Museum
(winemaking displays,
art exhibits).

NIEBAUM-COPPOLA ESTATE WINERY

**NIEBAUM-COPPOLA
ESTATE WINERY**
1991 St. Helena Hwy.
Rutherford, CA 94573
707-968-1100
800-RUBICON
info@niebaum-coppola.com
www.niebaum-coppola.com

OWNERS: Francis and
Eleanor Coppola.

LOCATION: About 3 miles
south of St. Helena via
Hwy. 29.

APPELLATION: Napa Valley.

HOURS: 10 A.M.–5 P.M.
daily; to 6 P.M., Friday
and Saturday, Memorial
Day–Labor Day.

TASTINGS: $7.50 for 4 wines;
$20 for 4 reserve wines.

TOURS: Chateau Tours and
tasting ($20); Vineyard
Tours and tasting ($20).
Call 707-968-1177 for
schedule.

THE WINES: Cabernet
Franc, Merlot, Pennino
Zinfandel, Rubicon;
Diamond Series
Chardonnay, Claret,
Merlot, Syrah; Director's
Series Cabernet
Sauvignon, Chardonnay,
Merlot, Sauvignon Blanc.

SPECIALTY: Rubicon
(Bordeaux blend).

WINEMAKER: Scott McLeod.

ANNUAL PRODUCTION:
200,000 cases.

OF SPECIAL NOTE: Film and
historic memorabilia on
display. Renting of model
sailboats ($1) for sailing
in pool. Shop including
extensive tabletop and
serving pieces and Italian
olive oils and other
condiments.

NEARBY ATTRACTIONS:
Silverado Museum
(Robert Louis Stevenson
memorabilia); Napa Valley
Museum (wine-making
displays, art exhibits).

For newcomers to the wine scene, the name of film director and producer Francis Ford Coppola may overshadow that of Gustave Niebaum, but from a historical perspective, the two are on equal footing. For all visitors, a chance to taste wine in a chateau built in the 1880s is a rare treat in itself, but the inclusion of a mini-museum of movie memorabilia offers an opportunity not to be missed.

If someone made a film about this winery, the establishing shot would undoubtedly be a lingering look at Niebaum's massive stone Inglenook Chateau. Niebaum was a Finnish sea captain who used the fortune he acquired in the Alaska fur trade to establish his winery in 1879. He succeeded in creating an estate worthy of the ones he had visited in Bordeaux. Fast forward to the 1970s. After a series of corporate ownerships, the winery had lost its reputation, its label, and a lot of vineyard land that was sold off piecemeal. Enter Francis Ford Coppola, who with his wife, Eleanor, began making wine at the old Niebaum winery in 1975. In 1995, they purchased the chateau and its adjacent vineyards, thereby reuniting the major parcels of the original estate.

Buying the property was just the beginning of Coppola's extensive project that, by 1997, restored and renovated the chateau and its grounds. In the European-style front courtyard, a redwood and stone pergola is graced with grapevines. Nearby, a ninety-by-thirty-foot reflecting pool is illuminated at night. During the day, children can rent elaborate wooden sailboats, reminiscent of those in the Luxembourg Gardens in Paris, to float in the shallow water.

Inside the chateau, the first thing visitors see is a grand staircase. Four master woodworkers labored for more than a year to build it from exotic hardwoods imported from Belize. At the top of the staircase is a large stained-glass window, Coppola's image of the reunification of this historic estate. In the second-floor museum, Don Corleone's desk and chair from *The Godfather*, costumes from Bram Stoker's *Dracula*, the 1948 car from *Tucker*, and Coppola's five Oscars are among the memorabilia on view. In the main lobby are two enormous tasting rooms where wines can be sampled at stand-up bars or at long tables. Also on the ground floor are displays of Coppola family photographs and mementos, as well as antique zoetropes and other artifacts from film history. Coppola pays homage to Niebaum not merely by giving him top billing. The Centennial Museum behind the staircase also relates the stories of the two immigrant families—Coppola is the son of Italian immigrants—who successfully pursued the American dream.

ROBERT MONDAVI WINERY

The one name most synonymous with fine California wine is Robert Mondavi. After more than half a century in the industry, Robert Mondavi has secured a place in history as the single most influential vintner in establishing the state as one of the premier winemaking regions in the world. Robert Mondavi built his winery in 1966, the first major winery to be opened in Napa Valley following the repeal of Prohibition in 1933. The mission-style architecture of this highly recognizable landmark is a tribute to the Spanish missionaries who brought wine to California and boasts the expansive archway and bell tower that are hallmarks of the designer, Cliff May. The winery is surrounded by the historic, 550-acre Tokalon Vineyard, originally planted in 1866 and now the backbone of Mondavi's Cabernet Sauvignon and Fumé Blanc.

Under the direction of winegrower Tim Mondavi, the winery completed its first major renovation in 2001. The new  state-of-the-art facility has oak fermenters and gentle gravity- flow handling for the creation and barrel aging of reserve and district red wines. The project also reorganized the layout of public spaces, making room for a gracious reception area, two inviting tasting rooms, and a spacious wine shop. Educational opportunities at the winery include a basic vineyard and winery tour with a wine-and-food tasting; extended vineyard and winegrowing tours; and various food-and-wine programs, some including lunch. The marriage of wine and food is celebrated daily in the Vineyard Room, a private dining room.

The winery's programs emphasize the presentation of wine in a broad cultural context. Robert Mondavi's wife, Margrit Biever, introduced the first winery culinary program, The Great Chefs at Robert Mondavi Winery, in 1976 and initiated two annual concert series and a fine arts gallery at the winery. She also worked closely with her husband to found COPIA: The American Center for Wine, Food and the Arts, which opened in Napa in 2001.

Robert Mondavi has spent a lifetime making wine in Napa Valley. After graduating from Stanford University in 1936, he joined his family in St. Helena before establishing his own winery. The family's goal has long been to produce wines that belong in the company of the great wines of the world. Great wines, they believe, reflect their origin, and the wines made at Robert Mondavi Winery express the *terroir* of the three vineyard properties that make up the winery's Napa Valley holdings in Oakville, Stags Leap District, and Carneros.

ROBERT MONDAVI WINERY
7801 St. Helena Hwy.
Oakville, CA 94562
707-968-2000
888-RMONDAVI
ext. 2000
info@robertmondavi.com
www.robertmondaviwinery.com

OWNERS: Robert Mondavi family.

LOCATION: About 16 miles north of Napa on Hwy. 29.

APPELLATIONS: Oakville and Napa Valley.

HOURS: 9 A.M.–5 P.M. daily.

TASTINGS: Limited-production and reserve wines in Tokalon Room; district and "Spotlight" wines from most distinctive Napa Valley vineyards in Appellation Room.

TOURS: Daily vineyard and winery tours with tasting ($10) at varying times beginning at 10 A.M.

THE WINES: Cabernet Sauvignon, Chardonnay, Fumé Blanc, Merlot, Pinot Noir, Sauvignon Blanc, Zinfandel.

SPECIALTY: Cabernet Sauvignon.

WINEMAKER: Tim Mondavi.

ANNUAL PRODUCTION: Unavailable.

OF SPECIAL NOTE: Extensive winery and vineyard tours, guided tastings, and food-and-wine pairings by reservation; Summer Jazz Festival and Winter Concert Festival plus other music and food events throughout year. Wine books and Italian imports in winery shop.

NEARBY ATTRACTIONS: Napa Valley Museum (wine-making displays, art exhibits); COPIA: The American Center for Wine, Food and the Arts.

RUTHERFORD HILL WINERY

RUTHERFORD HILL WINERY
200 Rutherford Hill Rd.
Rutherford, CA 94573
707-963-1871
info@rutherfordhill.com
www.rutherfordhill.com

OWNER: Anthony Terlato.

LOCATION: About 2 miles
south of St. Helena, just
north of Rutherford Cross
Rd. off Silverado Trail.

APPELLATION: Napa Valley.

HOURS: 10 A.M.–5 P.M. daily.

TASTINGS: $5 for 5 wines
and logo glass; $10 for
5 reserve wines and logo
glass.

TOURS: 11:30 A.M., 1:30 P.M.,
and 3:30 P.M. ($10);
includes tasting of 5 wines
and logo glass.

THE WINES: Cabernet
Sauvignon, Chardonnay,
Gewürztraminer, Merlot,
Port, Sangiovese, Sauvi-
gnon Blanc, Zinfandel.

SPECIALTIES: Merlot, Port,
Reserve Merlot, Zinfandel.

WINEMAKER:
David Dobson.

ANNUAL PRODUCTION:
100,000 cases.

OF SPECIAL NOTE: Picnic
areas with valley views.
Wine-blending seminars.
Some limited-production
wines sold only at winery.
Caves available for private
rental. Lila Jaeger's extra-
virgin olive oil and cookbooks by local authors
carried at winery shop.

NEARBY ATTRACTIONS:
Auberge du Soleil (hotel,
restaurant); Silverado
Museum (Robert Louis
Stevenson memorabilia).

Deep in a hillside east of the Silverado Trail lies a labyrinth of caves that extends nearly a mile. This subterranean facility is well suited for stashing thousands of barrels of wine that can age at fifty-eight to sixty degrees Fahrenheit and 85 percent humidity—ideal conditions for storing wine without the risk of evaporation that would occur in a less-humid environment. When the outside temperature spikes into the hundreds, all it takes is a major hosing down to set things right again.

A walk in the caves, which are redolent of red-wine aromas mingled with French and American oak, is a high point of a tour at Rutherford Hill. Built in 1984 at a cost of $1 million, the caves cover forty-four thousand square feet. They were the first ones in the Napa Valley created with mining technology rather than the hand labor used at other wineries during the nineteenth century.

Rutherford Hill is reached by Silverado Trail to a dead end in deluxe barn. The large redwood that extends nearly to the ground. beams anchor it in the so-called ing room, a dramatic two-story shades a large sunken courtyard in a narrow road leading up from the front of what looks like an ultra-structure has a steep-sloping roof Rough-hewn external support Rutherford dust. Outside the tast-arbor of wisteria vines partially springtime. It was the Rutherford dust that attracted a series of owners who realized the fine, rust-colored soil bore similarities to that of Bordeaux's Pomerol region, home to some of the world's finest Merlot.

The "barn," built by renowned winemaker Joseph Phelps, houses the winery and tasting room. In 1976, the property was purchased by Bill Jaeger, whose late wife, Lila, was a pioneer in initiating Napa's olive oil craze. Olive oil is still made from the trees on the winery property. Jaeger converted the forty-acre vineyard on the hill below the winery to Merlot vines, which continue to produce grapes for the current owner, Anthony Terlato, who took over in 1996. Terlato and his family, realizing that growing their own grapes would be the key to creating consistently complex, high-quality wines, subsequently purchased 60 additional acres in the Rutherford District and also farm another 130 Napa acres under long-term contracts.

The Terlato family's involvement in the wine business began with Anthony's father, who owned one of Chicago's largest wine stores. Over time, Anthony Terlato became a leading importer and marketer of fine wines from around the world, including those from Rutherford Hill. Having their own winery was the next logical step in the family's marrying of smart business and the pleasures of a wine country lifestyle.

Welcome to
RUTHERFORD HILL

Cave Tours · Tasting · Sales · Daily from 10 to 5

SILVER OAK CELLARS

Fans of fine Cabernet Sauvignon line up hours in advance—sometimes even camping overnight—for the new release of each Silver Oak wine. The vigil has become something of a ritual for connoisseurs who want to be sure to take home some of the winery's hard-to-find bottles. During the early 1990s, on each semiannual release day in Napa Valley, just a handful of people waited for the winery doors to open, but as news of the extraordinary wine spread and the crowds grew larger, Silver Oak began serving espresso drinks and doughnuts to the early-morning crowds and passing hot hors d'oeuvres throughout the afternoon. Now each release day unfolds at both of the winery's estates, in Napa and Alexander Valleys, and many wine lovers plan vacations around the festive events.

The biggest attraction, of course, is what lies in the bottle. Silver Oak produces elegant Cabernet Sauvignons with fully developed flavors and seamless textures. The winemaking program combines meticulous vineyard practices, har-monious blending, and extensive aging in exclusively American oak barrels—followed by even more aging in bottles. When the wine reaches the consumer, it is a synergy of depth and delicacy.

The winery's success began with two visionary men, Ray Duncan and Justin Meyer. Duncan was an entrepreneur in Colorado before being lured to California in the 1960s to help a childhood friend work on a vineyard deal. Impressed with the potential for wines in the Napa and Alexander Valleys, he purchased 750 acres of pastures, orchards, and vine-yards within a year. In 1972, he formed a partnership with Meyer, a former Christian Brothers winemaker. Their work together lasted some thirty years, until Meyer sold his part of the winery to Duncan.

Today the Duncan family sustains the commitment to excellence that has been a hallmark of Silver Oak. Each of the two estates is devoted to an individual style of Cabernet Sauvignon. The Alexander Valley wine has a particularly soft and fruity character, while the somewhat bolder Napa Valley wine has firmer tannins, making it appropriate for longer cellar aging. Both estates welcome visitors. The Napa Valley winery, on the site of the old Keig Dairy in Oakville, features a massive stone building with a wood-paneled tasting room. The dairy building, which served as Silver Oak's first aging cellars, is still in use today, though a larger barrel room and state-of-the-art winemaking facilities have been added. The Alexander Valley winery has an airy tasting room and an inviting courtyard for relaxing and enjoying the leisurely pace of Sonoma County.

SILVER OAK CELLARS
Napa Valley:
915 Oakville Cross Rd.
Oakville, CA 94562
Alexander Valley:
24625 Chianti Rd.
Geyserville, CA 95441
800-273-8809
info@silveroak.com
www.silveroak.com

OWNER:
Raymond T. Duncan.

LOCATION: Napa Valley:
1.2 miles east of Hwy 29;
Alexander Valley: 7 miles
from Canyon Rd. exit off
U.S. 101 via Chianti Rd.

APPELLATIONS: Napa Valley
and Alexander Valley.

HOURS: 9 A.M.–4 P.M.
Monday–Saturday.

TASTINGS: $10 per wine.

TOURS: Appointment
recommended.

THE WINE: Cabernet
Sauvignon.

SPECIALTY: Cabernet
Sauvignon.

WINEMAKER:
Daniel Baron.

ANNUAL PRODUCTION:
50,000 cases.

OF SPECIAL NOTE: Purchase
limits on some bottles.
Release days are held
simultaneously at both
estates for each wine: Napa
Valley Cabernet on first
Saturday in February,
Alexander Valley Cabernet
on first Saturday in
August.

NEARBY ATTRACTIONS:
Napa Valley Museum
(winemaking displays, art
exhibits).

SILVERADO VINEYARDS

SILVERADO VINEYARDS
6121 Silverado Trail
Napa, CA 94575
707-257-1770
info@silveradovineyards.com
www.silveradovineyards.com

OWNERS: Miller family.

LOCATION: About 1 mile
east of Yountville.

APPELLATION: Napa Valley.

HOURS: 10:30 A.M.–5 P.M.
daily in summer; 11 A.M.–
4:30 P.M. daily in winter.

TASTINGS: $7 for 4 estate
wines and current-release
Sangiovese.

TOURS: By appointment.

THE WINES: Cabernet
Sauvignon, Chardonnay,
Merlot, Sangiovese,
Sauvignon Blanc.

SPECIALTIES: Limited
Reserve Cabernet
Sauvignon, Chardonnay,
Merlot.

WINEMAKERS: Jack Stuart
and Jon Emmerich.

ANNUAL PRODUCTION:
115,000 cases.

OF SPECIAL NOTE: Limited-
production wines available
only in tasting room.

NEARBY ATTRACTIONS: Napa
Valley Museum (wine-
making displays, art
exhibits).

A steep, curving driveway worthy of a ski slope leads to the spectacular site of Silverado Vineyards. On either side of the road, wildflowers cling to the hillside as if for dear life. Yet nothing compares to the dramatic sight of the winery itself, a vision in ocher and terra-cotta, stone and stucco, that brings Tuscany to mind.

Many a visitor has noticed that Napa bears more than a passing resemblance to the Italian countryside. In the early 1970s, members of the Walt Disney family—Lillian Disney, Diane Disney Miller, and Ron Miller—decided they loved visiting the Napa Valley so much that they might as well move there. They purchased two neighboring vineyards in the Stags Leap District and began fulfilling Diane Miller's goal: to "make something beautiful from this land." For the first few years, the Millers sold their grapes  to local vintners, who made gold-medal wines from them. Inspired by this success, they established Silverado Vineyards in 1981 and started construction on their own thirty-thousand- square-foot winery, which opened to the public for tours and tastings in 1987.

The Millers named their new winery after the long-vanished mining community that once thrived on the slopes of nearby Mount St. Helena. The name Silverado was made famous by author Robert Louis Stevenson, who lived there in the 1880s and wrote about the region in *The Silverado Squatters*.

Since its founding, the winery has acquired three more vineyards and now farms more than three hundred acres. Some of those vineyards, notably ninety-five acres of Cabernet Sauvignon and Merlot, are visible from the terrace on the second floor. Visitors can sip their wine at small glass-topped tables, which sit on a floor made of cobblestones that once graced New York City streets. If you look closely, you can see that some of the stones are worn smooth, while others are set bottom side up, with their still-rough surfaces showing. Only a low wall separates the terrace from the abundant vines and wildflowers that bloom at different times of the year.

The adjacent four-thousand-square-foot tasting room opened in 2000, replacing the much smaller original tasting room in another part of the building. Huge picture windows on two sides offer north-facing panoramas of vineyards and the hilly Stags Leap landscape. Antique beams of Douglas fir imported from a timber mill in British Columbia crisscross the ceiling. Overall, the design is sleek and contemporary, free of cluttering knickknacks. Across the hall, French doors provide a view of the temperature-controlled barrel cellar. There is no access to the cellar from here, but a small sign invites visitors to open the doors and inhale the heady aroma.

ST. CLEMENT VINEYARDS

Rows of vineyards march up the slope to a fetching olive-green structure that was obviously built as a private residence. Fritz H. Rosenbaum, a German stained-glass merchant, and his wife, Johanna, built this Gothic-Victorian–style home for their family in 1878. His plans included a properly equipped wine cellar where he could make wines as he had in the old country. Thanks to those first wines from the stone cellars beneath the house, Johannaberg Cellars became one of the earliest commercial wineries in the Napa Valley. Nearly a century and a half later, the original cellars are used to house some of the thirty thousand cases that St. Clement produces annually.

The pleasant walkway up from the parking lot is rimmed with towering white and pink oleander bushes, which give way to hydrangeas and roses. As an extra bit of charm, tiny blossoming ground-cover plants have gained toeholds in the crevices of the old stone retaining wall in front of the historic home.

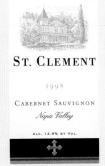

The Rosenbaums situated their house to take advantage of a 180-degree view of the Vaca Range to the east. Visitors can enjoy the same vista from a charming swing on the front porch or from the stone patio nearby. Here small tables for two are set in the shade of fir and poplar trees. The patio is rimmed on two sides by a low stone wall and on the other two by a short, old-fashioned wrought-iron fence. In the center is a fountain encircled by fragrant star jasmine. The entire property would make a lovely restaurant if it weren't such a success as a winery.

St. Clement hasn't been a winery all these decades. After Fritz Rosenbaum's death in 1893, the grand residence was sold to the first of several families who lived in it until the middle of the twentieth century. By the 1940s, the house had fallen into disrepair. It was rehabilitated and restored in 1962 by Michael and Shirley Robbins, who established the property as Spring Mountain Vineyards in 1968.

The home changed hands again in 1975, when Dr. and Mrs. William Casey purchased it and christened their first wines St. Clement Vineyards. Their releases until 1979 consisted of small quantities of Cabernet Sauvignon and Chardonnay. Then they built a modern stone winery to accommodate up to ten thousand cases. Although the winery changed hands again and again, the Victorian remained a private home. In 1991, it was remodeled once more and welcomed the public to tastings and open houses. Eight years later, it was purchased by Beringer (now Beringer Blass Wine Estates). The specialty is still small lots of ultrapremium wines made from Napa Valley grapes.

ST. CLEMENT VINEYARDS
2867 Hwy. 29 North
St. Helena, CA 94574
800-331-8266
info@stclement.com
www.stclement.com

OWNER: Beringer Blass Wine Estates.

LOCATION: North side of St. Helena.

APPELLATION: Napa Valley.

HOURS: 10 A.M.–4 P.M. daily.

TASTINGS: $5 for 5 wines.

TOURS: By appointment.

THE WINES: Cabernet Sauvignon, Chardonnay, Merlot, Sauvignon Blanc.

SPECIALTY: Cabernet Sauvignon.

WINEMAKER: Aaron Pott.

ANNUAL PRODUCTION: 30,000 cases.

OF SPECIAL NOTE: Picnic tables available by reservation only for parties of up to 15 people.

NEARBY ATTRACTIONS: Bothe-Napa State Park (hiking, picnicking, horseback riding, swimming Memorial Day–Labor Day); Bale Grist Mill State Historic Park (water-powered mill circa 1846); Silverado Museum (Robert Louis Stevenson memorabilia).

St. Supéry Vineyards and Winery

St. Supéry Vineyards and Winery
8440 St. Helena Hwy.
Rutherford, CA 94573
800-942-0809, ext. 44;
707-963-4507
divinecab@stsupery.com
www.stsupery.com

Owners: Skalli family.

Location: About 4 miles south of St. Helena via Hwy. 29.

Appellation: Napa Valley.

Hours: 10 a.m.–5 p.m. daily, November–April; 10 a.m.–5:30 p.m. daily, May–October.

Tastings: $5 (lifetime tasting pass) for 5 or more wines; $10 for 3 reserve wines.

Tours: 11 a.m., 1 p.m., and 3 p.m. Self-guided tours during operating hours.

The Wines: Cabernet Franc, Cabernet Sauvignon, Chardonnay, Merlot, Moscato, Red and White Meritage, Sauvignon Blanc, Semillon, single-vineyard wines.

Specialties: Cabernet Sauvignon, Sauvignon Blanc.

Winemaker: Michael Beaulac.

Annual Production: 120,000 cases.

Of Special Note: Changing art exhibitions; winemaking exhibits in Wine Discovery Center. Barrel tastings and blending seminars. Vineyard-designated and small lots available only at winery; some bottle limits on library wines. Shop selling condiments and other goods from Provence.

Nearby Attractions: Napa Valley Museum (winemaking displays, art exhibits); Silverado Museum (Robert Louis Stevenson memorabilia).

The idea is so simple that it's a wonder no one else thought of it sooner. St. Supéry's Wine Discovery Center has an ingenious hands-on exhibit called "Smellavision" that helps visitors learn to identify various aromas found in wine. If you want to experience the scents of cedar and black cherry that characterize Cabernet Sauvignon, for instance, or the aroma of freshly cut grass associated with Sauvignon Blanc, just press a button, and the display delivers a whiff of the real thing. When you get to the tasting room, those olfactory memories will still be fresh in your mind.

The Wine Discovery Center also educates visitors about how vines grow and how wines are made. Panoramic murals and museum-quality exhibits and models depict the Napa Valley climate and geology, key factors in the creation of the region's world-class wines. Self-guided tours of the winery include stops at various production stations and a one-acre living vineyard.

Robert Skalli, after managing the family's wine business in France, made frequent trips to the Napa Valley during the 1970s. 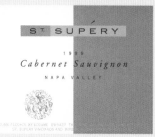 Those visits convinced him that his family's experience in the European food industry could translate into a viable California wine business. After researching vineyards and consulting Napa's most respected vintners, Skalli chose a fifteen-hundred-acre property in nearby Pope Valley, where vineyards had been planted nearly a century earlier. In 1982, the Skalli family purchased the working Dollarhide cattle ranch and began replanting it with high-quality grapevines. Although the family subsequently acquired other vineyards, the delicate fruitiness and light body of the Dollarhide grapes continue to imbue St. Supéry's wine with a distinctive style.

The Skallis established the St. Supéry winery in 1986 on a fifty-six-acre parcel that had once been part of George Yount's Mexican land grant, Rancho Caymus. The property was developed in the late nineteenth century by Louis and Joseph Atkinson, accomplished Philadelphia clothiers who came to San Francisco during the Gold Rush and later migrated to the Napa Valley. Joseph became a successful vintner but lost his property after his vineyards were destroyed by *Phylloxera*, a root louse. Winemaker Edward St. Supéry took over the Atkinson property, and the Skallis decided to name their winery after him. The vineyards were replanted with phylloxera-resistant rootstock in 1957.

The Atkinsons' Queen Anne Victorian home is the first feature visitors see as they approach the winery. Built in 1882, it is on the National Register of Historic Places. The pretty white building was restored by noted museum designer Gordon Ashby and now offers displays that give visitors a sense of vintner life more than a century ago.

STERLING VINEYARDS

Travelers in the upper Napa Valley often get out their cameras as soon as they see the striking white buildings atop a three-hundred-foot forested knoll south of Calistoga. Even more camera worthy is the journey to the winery via aerial tram. Cars and worries are left behind as visitors glide up the hill. The winery's designer, inspired by Napa's Mediterranean climate, intentionally modeled Sterling on the style of architecture on the photogenic Greek island of Mykonos.

The winery also stands out for its self-guided tours, which allow visitors to explore the facility from elevated platforms that feature educational graphics showing the entire winemaking process. The tour culminates on a terrace offering a commanding view of the Napa Valley. Upon entering the main tasting room, guests are greeted with a complimentary glass of Sauvignon Blanc, then are

shown to a table where the staff serves a choice of current releases. Visitors can enjoy the comfortable surroundings, or in warm weather sit on a patio with a view of the Bay Area's highest mountain, 4,344-foot Mt. St. Helena. Displayed throughout the tasting rooms is a collection of wine art and artifacts spanning five centuries.

Sterling was established in 1969 with the purchase of fifty vineyard acres by Englishman and international paper broker Peter Newton. In 2002, the winery completed a $14 million renovation, which included three new tasting rooms—one for the public, another for reserve wines, and yet another for Cellar Club members. Sterling has purchased a number of vineyards over the decades and now farms twelve hundred acres in the Napa Valley. These properties vary widely in topography, soil types, and microclimates, from the very steep Diamond Mountain Ranch west of Calistoga to the rolling hills around Winery Lake in the southern Carneros near San Francisco Bay. The winery also acquires grapes from other sources. One is the prestigious Three Palms Vineyard just southeast of the winery and owned by Sloan Upton, Sterling's first vineyard manager, and his brother John. The vineyard's stately palms were planted in the late 1800s by then-landowner Lilly Hitchcock Coit, best known for building San Francisco's Coit Tower.

When the winery was established, the owners were confident about the future of Cabernet Sauvignon, but took a chance on three then-unproven varietals—Sauvignon Blanc, Chardonnay, and Merlot—by including them in early vineyard plantings. Consequently, in 1969, Sterling Vineyards became the first American producer of a vintage-dated Napa Valley Merlot.

STERLING VINEYARDS
1111 Dunaweal Ln.
Calistoga, CA 94515
707-942-3344, 800-726-6136
info@sterlingvineyards.com
www.sterlingvineyards.com

OWNER: Diageo Chateau & Estate Wines.

LOCATION: Just south of Calistoga between Hwy. 29 and Silverado Trail.

APPELLATION: Napa Valley.

HOURS: 10:30 A.M.–4:30 P.M. daily.

TASTINGS: $10 for 4 wines (includes aerial tram).

TOURS: Self-guided tours available during operating hours. Groups by appointment.

THE WINES: Cabernet Sauvignon, Chardonnay, Malvasia Bianca, Merlot, Muscat Canelli, Pinot Gris, Pinot Noir, Sangiovese, Sauvignon Blanc, Syrah, Viognier, Zinfandel.

SPECIALTIES: Vineyard-designated Chardonnay, Pinot Noir, Merlot, and Cabernet Sauvignon; reserve Chardonnay, Merlot, and Cabernet Sauvignon.

WINEMAKERS: Rob Hunter and Greg Fowler.

ANNUAL PRODUCTION: 400,000 cases.

OF SPECIAL NOTE: Children are given juice, crayons, and note-cards to color. Annual events include Merlot in May. Ten wines made for Cellar Club members available to general public only at winery. Historic collection of wine art and artifacts on display year-round. Shop featuring 19th-century British sterling silver antiques.

NEARBY ATTRACTIONS: Bothe-Napa State Park; Robert Louis Stevenson State Park; hot-air balloon rides; Old Faithful Geyser of California; Petrified Forest; Sharpsteen Museum (exhibits on Robert Louis Stevenson and Walt Disney animator Ben Sharpsteen).

SWANSON VINEYARDS AND WINERY

SWANSON VINEYARDS AND WINERY
1271 Manley Ln.
Rutherford, CA 94573
707-967-3500
salon@swansonvineyards.com
www.swansonvineyards.com

OWNER:
W. Clarke Swanson, Jr.

LOCATION: .5 mile west of Hwy. 29.

APPELLATION: Napa Valley.

HOURS: By appointment, Wednesday–Sunday, 11 A.M., 1:30 P.M., and 4 P.M.

TASTINGS: $25 for 4 wines; $40 for 7 wines.

TOURS: None.

THE WINES: Alexis (Cabernet Sauvignon blend), Angelica, Cabernet Sauvignon, Late-Harvest Semillon, Merlot, Petite Sirah, Pinot Grigio, Rosato, Sangiovese, sparkling Muscat, Syrah.

SPECIALTIES: Alexis, Merlot.

WINEMAKER:
Marco Cappelli.

ANNUAL PRODUCTION: 25,000 cases.

OF SPECIAL NOTE: Number of guests limited to 8. Angelica, Cabernet Sauvignon, Rosato, Sangiovese, Late-Harvest Semillon, and Petite Sirah available only at winery.

NEARBY ATTRACTIONS: Silverado Museum (Robert Louis Stevenson memorabilia); Napa Valley Museum (winemaking displays, art exhibits).

Time seems to stand still when you step inside the Salon at Swanson. Or maybe the Salon takes you back to an earlier era of leisure, luxury, and lingering conversation. For one hour at least, visitors can forget the outside world and concentrate on the wine and their fellow tasters. Only eight people are seated at each tasting session. Surrounded by fine things and served one wine after another, visitors are guided by the "salonnier" through that day's menu of wines, accompanied by little plates of elegant cheeses and crackers and capped with a bonbon made exclusively for Swanson, paired with the final wine.

At the appointed hour, arriving visitors are welcomed by the host into the stucco winery with its weathered blue window shutters. The fantasy begins when they step into an intimate, intensely decorated room with coral-colored walls adorned by seventeen colorful paintings, some as tall as eight feet, by noted Bay Area figurative artist Ira Yeager. Together, they make up his Vintage Peasant series, most of the works having been created especially for this room. Then it is time to take a seat at an octagonal table made of Moroccan wood inlaid with agate. A small menu lists the day's offerings, which are already arranged on the table. Always among them are wines available only at the winery.

According to Alexis Swanson Farrer, director of marketing, the salon concept coalesced in 2000 as an expression of the Swanson family's affinity for an old-fashioned way of life. "It's all about service and intimacy and obsessive attention to detail," she says. "Every tasting is like a little cocktail party held in each guest's honor. The common thread is a love of wine, but the conversation is never technical. It's all a balance of humor and whimsy, art and theater." One look around the jewel box of a room proves her point. Details of the decor may change slightly over the years, but the style, established by noted New York interior designer Tom Britt, does not.

Catering to the traveler looking for the less attainable, the Salon offers such small-batch wines as Angelica, Rosato, Sangiovese, Old Vine Syrah, Late-Harvest Semillon, Cabernet Sauvignon, and a sparkling Muscat—wines found only at the Swanson Salon.

WILLIAM HILL WINERY

Perched on the crest of a hill in the southern Napa Valley, this two-hundred-acre estate seems miles away from civilization. From the tasting room, visitors see the rolling landscape to the north and the Mayacamas Range to the west. Hillside vineyards completely surround the winery, creating a serene setting. William Hill Winery is a bit off the beaten track, since few wineries are found in this part of Napa. Wine lovers seeking an intimate experience will appreciate the refreshing change of pace from the larger wineries farther up the valley.

The winery farms 140 acres on the Silverado Bench, named for the terracelike land formation

east of the Silverado Trail. This rocky, hilly region runs south from Oak Knoll Avenue to Trancas/Monticello Road. Like the adjacent Stags Leap District, the rugged Silverado Bench produces intensely flavored Cabernet Sauvignon and Merlot grapes with soft tannins and pronounced berry flavors. Each of these varietals has defined William Hill's elegant style since 1978. The distinctive characteristics of the property are apparent in the Napa Valley Cabernet Sauvignon, Napa Valley Merlot, and Reserve Napa Valley Cabernet Sauvignon. The winery also produces two Chardonnays from its eighty acres of vineyards in Carneros, an appellation known for intense flavors of apple, pear, and tropical fruit. Pinot Blanc, from the Atlas Peak appellation, is a small-production wine available exclusively in the Tasting Room.

Winemaker Tina Mitchell has been part of the winemaking team since 1991 and has been an integral part of its winemaking regimes. Educated in enology at the University of California at Davis, she spent three years at Louis Martini and nearly six years at Niebaum-Coppola, where she worked closely with Beaulieu's legendary winemaker André Tchelistcheff. "Andre was a real stickler for quality," Mitchell notes, "and paid close attention to the smallest of housekeeping details. He was a wonderful example of how hands-on a really good winemaker has to be. André had a huge influence on my approach to winemaking."

The tasting room features a gleaming oak bar and, behind it, huge windows that overlook the barrel room and offer a glimpse of the winemaking team at work. Tall chairs flank square tables for visitors who prefer to settle in and relax awhile. The winery's pastoral setting is enhanced by gardens of seasonal flowers and a fountain surrounded by raised beds of rosemary and other aromatic herbs. To the west, an arbor opens to a lawn area and rose garden. A garden path leads to a trellis-covered patio with sweeping views of the Napa Valley.

WILLIAM HILL WINERY
1761 Atlas Peak Rd.
Napa, California 94558
707-224-4477
whw_info@williamhillwinery.com
www.williamhillwinery.com

OWNER: Allied Domecq Wines USA.

LOCATION: About 5 miles north of Napa, via Silverado Trail, Hardman Ave., and Atlas Peak Rd.

APPELLATION: Napa Valley.

HOURS: 10:30 A.M.–4 P.M. daily.

TASTINGS: $5 for 4 or 5 wines; $20 for sit-down cheese and Aura Experience tasting (by appointment).

TOURS: By appointment.

THE WINES: Cabernet Sauvignon, Chardonnay, Merlot, Pinot Blanc.

SPECIALTY: Aura, limited-production 100 percent Cabernet Sauvignon.

WINEMAKER: Tina Mitchell.

ANNUAL PRODUCTION: Unavailable.

OF SPECIAL NOTE: Pinot Blanc sold only at tasting room.

NEARBY ATTRACTIONS: Restaurants and occasional professional golf tournaments at Silverado Country Club; COPIA: The American Center for Wine, Food and the Arts.

ZD WINES

ZD WINES
8383 Silverado Trail
Napa, CA 94558
800-487-7757
info@zdwines.com
www.zdwines.com

OWNERS: deLeuze family.

LOCATION: About 2.5 miles south of Zinfandel Ln.

APPELLATION: Rutherford.

HOURS: 10 A.M.–4:30 P.M. daily.

TASTINGS: $5 for current releases; $10 for 2 reserve wines.

TOURS: By appointment.

THE WINES: Abacus (solera-style blend of ZD Reserve Cabernet Sauvignon), Cabernet Sauvignon, Chardonnay, Merlot, Pinot Noir.

SPECIALTY: Chardonnay.

WINEMAKERS: Robert deLeuze, wine master; Chris Pisani, winemaker.

ANNUAL PRODUCTION: 30,000 cases.

OF SPECIAL NOTE: Sit-down wine and cheese seminars on Saturday and Sunday by appointment ($20; maximum 10 people).

NEARBY ATTRACTIONS: Bothe-Napa State Park (hiking, picnicking, horseback riding, swimming Memorial Day–Labor Day); Bale Grist Mill State Historic Park (water-powered mill circa 1846); Silverado Museum (Robert Louis Stevenson memorabilia).

The entrance to this family-owned winery is intended to slow visitors to a leisurely wine-country pace. Essentially, it is a long garden path whose narrow confines impart an intimate feel. Azaleas and camellias thrive in the light shade of grapevines suspended from an arbor. Large wooden doors open into a high-ceilinged tasting room with a beautiful rounded-oak and bubinga tasting bar that resembles a wooden wine tank, where the friendly staff pours wine for guests.

Founding partner Norman deLeuze, having developed a passion for great red and white Burgundy, set out to produce similar wines in California using the classic Pinot Noir and Chardonnay varietals. It has been said that winemaking isn't rocket science, but in fact deLeuze had been designing liquid rocket engines at Aerojet-General in Sacramento, where he met his original partner Gino Zepponi. But what would they name their new enterprise? Aerojet had a quality-control program called Zero De-

fects, and posters hung around the facility displayed a ZD logo. This matched the partners' initials and created a new association for the letters ZD, what is today a well-known Rutherford winery. In 1969, they started out by purchasing grapes from Winery Lake Vineyard in southern Sonoma's Carneros region. The 1969 Pinot Noir had the distinction of being the first wine to be labeled with the Carneros designation. The first ZD Chardonnay was made in 1972.

Eventually, deLeuze turned to winemaking full-time, while his wife, Rosa Lee, handled sales and marketing. They purchased six acres, built their own winery, and planted Cabernet Sauvignon in Rutherford in 1979. This established a three-varietal focus for the winery: Chardonnay, Pinot Noir, and Cabernet Sauvignon. Four years later, Robert deLeuze was named winemaker. He had been working in ZD's cellars since age twelve, learning through hands-on experience, and later studied at the University of California at Davis. His full-time involvement with ZD's winemaking for twenty-three years ensured a consistency in winemaking style. Over the years, ZD wines have graced the tables of White House dinner parties spanning three administrations. The deLeuze family has been crafting California wines for more than three decades. The winery is owned and operated by Norman, Rosa Lee, and their three adult children: Robert as wine master, Brett as marketing director, and Julie as administrative director. Robert's two children, Brandon and Jill, began working summers and holidays at ZD in their early teens, bringing a third generation to this family affair.

SONOMA

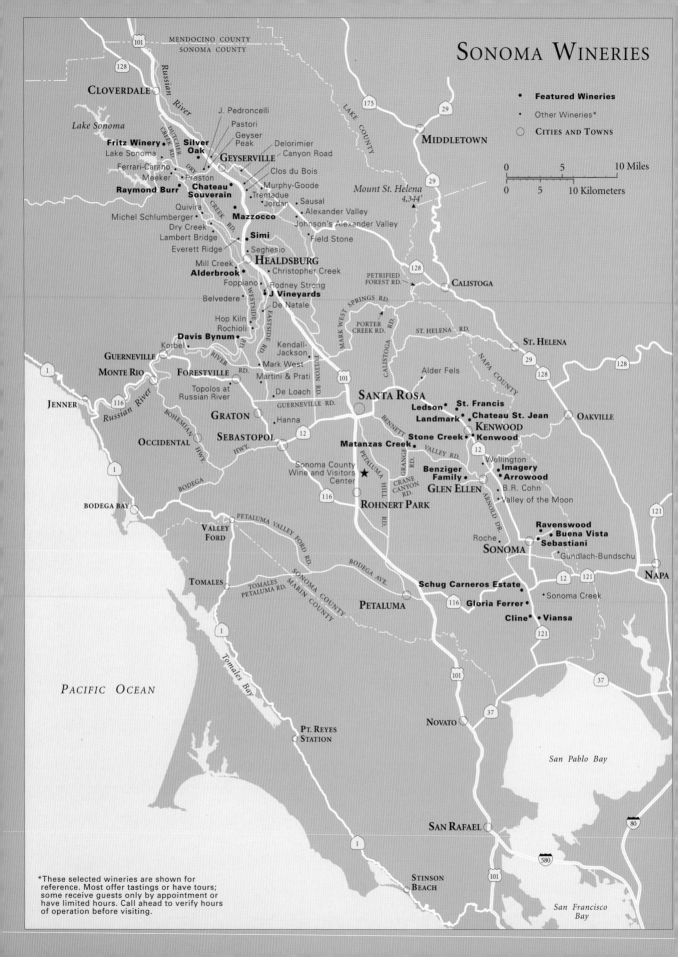

Sonoma boasts the most geographical diversity and the highest number of appellations in wine country. From the Pacific Coast to the inland valleys, to the Mayacamas Range that defines the border with Napa County, the countryside is crisscrossed by rural roads, making it an ideal destination for casual exploration.

Most of the county's oldest wineries, including Buena Vista and Sebastiani, can be found around the historic town of Sonoma. Facing the eight-acre central plaza are nineteenth-century adobe and false-front buildings that now house shops, restaurants, inns, and historic sights. Diverse luminaries, such as the horticulturist Luther Burbank and the cartoonist Charles Schulz of "Peanuts" fame, made their homes in Santa Rosa; no trip would be complete without visiting the museums named for them. North and west of Santa Rosa, the Russian River wends its way to the coast, offering boating, swimming, and fishing opportunities and the shade of giant redwoods along its banks.

Healdsburg, which has quickly evolved from a quiet backwater to the hottest destination in the county, is at the hub of three major grape-growing regions—Russian River Valley, Alexander Valley, and Dry Creek Valley—all within a ten-minute drive of the town plaza.

ALDERBROOK VINEYARDS AND WINERY

Location, location, location. It's as important in the winery business as it is in residential real estate. Sun, wind, fog, drainage, altitude, exposure, soil type, and other considerations are the stuff of appellations. Some wineries, including Alderbrook Vineyards, get the best of two worlds.

The winery is situated at the southernmost tip of Dry Creek Valley and in close proximity to the Russian River Valley to the south. As a result, the Alderbrook vineyards receive the typically intense afternoon heat of Dry Creek but also some of the blessings of the ocean air that chills the Russian River Valley with the approach of evening. As the mass of air creeps up the valley from the Pacific Ocean, it produces fog in the evening and early morning. After ripening all day in the summer sunshine, the grapes are cooled down at night, giving them valuable extra time on the vines. The winery credits this extended "hang time" with providing a smooth evolution for the fruit as it develops rich, full-bodied characteristics.

When it comes to growing grapes, the right location can be a matter of mere yards. As winemaker Thomas "T. J." Evans says, even vineyards located just one hundred yards apart and planted with identical vines and rootstock can produce wines with distinctly different flavors. Evans, who came to Alderbrook in 2000 from La Crema Winery, spends most of his time in the vineyards trying to anticipate what they will produce, especially in regard to the winery's reserve Zinfandels. Whereas all wine grapes mature unevenly to some extent, Zinfandel is the most notorious for having clusters that contain berries in differing stages of ripeness, and Evans finds there's no substitute for personal inspection of the grapes from bud to harvest.

Sauvignon Blanc, Chardonnay, and Merlot are also produced from the estate vineyards. In addition to the fruit grown on its sixty-five-acre estate, the winery has agreements with top growers in both the Dry Creek Valley and the Russian River Valley appellations. Alderbrook's Pinot Noir comes from the latter, which is world renowned for this varietal.

The winery is a low-key complex of understated buildings that reminds one of the French countryside. White paint trims the edges of the balcony around the wide veranda, and an area of lush green grass beckons picnickers, who can buy deli items in the spacious tasting room. Recently renovated and enlarged, the tasting room also offers a separate "VIP" tasting room, where the winery conducts food-and-wine pairing seminars hosted by the winemaker and the winery chef. Alderbrook prides itself on its knowledgeable staff who further enhance guests' experience.

ALDERBROOK VINEYARDS AND WINERY
2306 Magnolia Dr.
Healdsburg, CA 95448
707-433-5987
800-405-5987
info@alderbrook.com
www.alderbrook.com

OWNER:
Terlato Wine Group.

LOCATION: Off Westside Rd. west of Healdsburg and U.S. 101.

APPELLATION: Dry Creek Valley.

HOURS: 10 A.M.–5 P.M. daily.

TASTINGS: Complimentary for 4 wines.

TOURS: Contact winery for details.

THE WINES: Cabernet Sauvignon, Carignane, Chardonnay, Gewürztraminer, Merlot, Pinot Noir, Sauvignon Blanc, Zinfandel.

SPECIALTIES: Dry Creek Zinfandel, Estate Chardonnay and Sauvignon Blanc, Russian River Pinot Noir, vineyard-designated reserve Zinfandels.

WINEMAKER: T. J. Evans.

ANNUAL PRODUCTION: 30,000 cases.

OF SPECIAL NOTE: Picnic items stocked in wine shop; picnicking allowed on veranda.

NEARBY ATTRACTIONS: Russian River (swimming, canoe and kayak rentals).

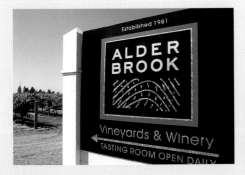

ARROWOOD VINEYARDS & WINERY

ARROWOOD VINEYARDS & WINERY
14347 Hwy. 12
Glen Ellen, CA 95442
707-935-2600
hospitality@
arrowoodvineyards.com
www.arrowoodvineyards.com

FOUNDERS: Richard and Alis Arrowood.

LOCATION: About 3 miles north of town of Sonoma via Hwy 12.

APPELLATION: Sonoma Valley.

HOURS: 10:00 A.M.–4:30 P.M. daily.

TASTINGS: $5 for 4 wines; $10 for 4 reserve wines.

TOURS: 10:30 A.M. and 2:30 P.M. daily by appointment.

THE WINES: Cabernet Sauvignon, Chardonnay, Gewürztraminer, Malbec, Merlot, Pinot Blanc, Riesling (late harvest), Syrah, Viognier.

SPECIALTY: All wines are made from Sonoma County grapes.

WINEMAKER: Richard Arrowood.

ANNUAL PRODUCTION: 30,000 cases.

OF SPECIAL NOTE: Occasional wine dinners; extended winery/cellar tours by appointment; annual Chardonnay in May event. Wine accessories and gift packs sold at winery shop.

NEARBY ATTRACTIONS: Jack London State Historic Park (museum, hiking, horseback riding); Sonoma Valley Regional Park (hiking, dog park).

From the highway, the pair of gray, New England farmhouse–style buildings with generous porches neatly trimmed in white could easily pass for a country inn. In fact, the property was originally intended to become a bed-and-breakfast, but it never opened for business. Today, these handsome, sedate structures are home to the Arrowood Winery. The sweeping view from the wide porches encompasses the Arrowood vineyards, a neighboring winery, and the oak-studded slopes of Sonoma Mountain on the western horizon.

Richard Arrowood made his name as the longtime winemaker at Chateau St. Jean, just up the road in Kenwood. A native San Franciscan raised in Santa Rosa, he earned degrees in organic chemistry and enology, and got his start in the business in 1965 at Korbel Champagne Cellars. In 1974, the founders of Chateau St. Jean hired Arrowood as their first employee. For the next sixteen years, he made wines that earned both him and the winery worldwide attention. His reputation as one of the country's best  winemakers was firmly established with his late-harvest Riesling, a varietal that he produces today under his own label.

In the late 1980s, he met and married Alis Demers, who had been working in the wine industry since 1978. Together, they began establishing the Arrowood brand. They found the perfect ten-acre property and designed their winery to blend harmoniously with the rural landscape. When they realized that they had inherited two donkeys, Burt and Ernie, from the previous landowner, they lacked the heart to kick them out and fenced off an area behind the winery.

While Richard was still at Chateau St. Jean, Alis was topping barrels or running the bottling line when she wasn't giving tours and conducting tastings. Richard began working full-time at the winery in 1990, freeing Alis to devote her energies to sales and marketing. Richard began by focusing exclusively on reserve-quality Chardonnay and Cabernet Sauvignon. Before long, he was seduced by the idea of working with less common varietals, particularly when he found exceptional fruit. Today Arrowood produces Malbec, for instance, as well as more familiar wines, all made from Sonoma County grapes. In 1998, the winery realized a long-cherished dream: opening a spacious Hospitality House next door. The building has a dramatic vaulted ceiling, an enormous stone fireplace flanked by comfortable seating, and a second-floor loft for private events. Picture windows afford magnificent views of Sonoma Valley. Visitors are welcome to walk out the huge glass doors and relax on the wraparound veranda, wineglasses in hand.

BENZIGER FAMILY WINERY

The Benziger Family Winery is laid out on a particularly picturesque hillside of Sonoma Mountain. In this storybook setting extolled by adventure author Jack London, the Benzigers have created both an award-winning winery and a lifestyle that many would envy. Their grape-growing practices and other innovations have earned the winery kudos far and wide. The Benzigers like to share their property with visitors. The eighty-five acres of estate vineyards are accessible daily on forty-five-minute Vineyard Tram Tours. Hauled by a tractor, the tram full of passengers is treated to a close look at the grapes, breathtaking views of Sonoma Mountain, a short course in site-specific farming, and a chance to sip a little fruit of the vine.

None of this would be possible if Mike Benziger had not followed his instincts up a narrow country road between Glen Ellen and Jack London's old Beauty Ranch. There he stumbled across a 140-year-old farmhouse—and promptly knew it was where he wanted to establish his winery. Mike's father, Bruno, was a well-established wine importer in New York, and, like most of his six siblings, Mike had done a stint in the family business. In 1981, Bruno helped Mike and his wife, Mary, purchase the property, which was to become the original Glen Ellen Winery. In short order, the elder Benzigers followed their son, as did Mike's six siblings.

Throughout the 1980s, the Benzigers enjoyed great success building the Glen Ellen brand. In 1993, the family shifted its focus to ultrapremium wines. They sold the Glen Ellen label—but not the vineyards or the winery—and established the Benziger Family Winery on the same site. The winery currently uses three hundred lots of grapes from more than sixty ranches in more than a dozen appellations. At their property and in concert with outside growers, the Benzigers practice extensive site-specific farming techniques such as canopy manipulation to alter and maximize desirable flavors. For example, if a Cabernet Sauvignon vineyard consistently produces the green olive flavors associated with cool temperatures and low light, increasing the vine's exposure to sunlight by reducing the canopy would result in more heat and more desirable blackberry, chocolate, or minty flavors. Over the years, such small but steady innovations have proven successful in maximizing the potential flavor intensity for each vineyard. The Benziger family story may not be Jack London material, but you can't beat it for a happy ending.

BENZIGER FAMILY WINERY
1883 London Ranch Rd.
Glen Ellen, CA 95442
888-490-2739
greatwine@benziger.com
www.benziger.com

OWNERS: Benziger family.

LOCATION: 1 mile west of Glen Ellen via London Ranch Rd.

APPELLATION: Sonoma Mountain.

HOURS: 10 A.M.–5 P.M. daily.

TASTINGS: Complimentary for many wines; $5 for 5 limited-production wines; $10 for 5 wines in Private Estate Wine Room.

TOURS: Vineyard Tram Tours ($5) and self-guided tours.

THE WINES: Cabernet Sauvignon, Chardonnay, Fumé Blanc, Merlot, Muscat Canelli, Pinot Noir, Sauvignon Blanc, Syrah, Zinfandel.

SPECIALTIES: Vineyard-designated and reserve wines.

WINEMAKER: Terry Nolan.

ANNUAL PRODUCTION: 165,000 cases.

OF SPECIAL NOTE: Estate and limited-production wines available only at winery caves. Picnic area in redwood grove; children's play area; peacock aviary; display of antique farm and winery equipment. Wine accessories, home furnishings, and cookbooks at winery shop.

NEARBY ATTRACTIONS: Jack London State Historic Park (museum, hiking, horseback riding); Sonoma Valley Regional Park (hiking, dog park); Morton's Sonoma Springs Resort (swimming, picnicking).

BUENA VISTA CARNEROS ESTATE WINERY

BUENA VISTA CARNEROS ESTATE WINERY
18000 Old Winery Rd.
Sonoma, CA 95476
707-265-1472
bvw_info@buenavistawinery.com
www.buenavistawinery.com

OWNER: Allied Domecq Wines USA.

LOCATION: About 2 miles east of Sonoma Plaza.

APPELLATION: Carneros.

HOURS: 10 A.M.–5 P.M. daily.

TASTINGS: $5 for 4 wines.

TOURS: Self-guided tours and historical tours during operating hours.

THE WINES: Cabernet Sauvignon, Chardonnay, Cream Sherry, Merlot, Pinot Noir, Port, Sauvignon Blanc, Zinfandel, Zinfandel Rosé.

SPECIALTIES: Cabernet Sauvignon, Chardonnay, Pinot Noir.

WINEMAKER: Judy Matulich-Weitz.

ANNUAL PRODUCTION: 315,000 cases.

OF SPECIAL NOTE: Picnic tables. Several specialties available only at winery. Shop offering wine books and picnic fare. Art gallery and artists' discussions. Shakespeare by local Avalon Players on Sunday evenings in August and September.

NEARBY ATTRACTIONS: Mission San Francisco Solano and other historic buildings in downtown Sonoma; Vella Cheese Company; Sonoma Cheese Factory; Train Town (rides for children); bike rentals.

Millions have made the pilgrimage to California's oldest premium winery since it was founded in 1857. For many, it was their first visit to a winery. While new wineries continue to open every year in Northern California, they cannot compete with Buena Vista's unmistakable cachet as the first in the state. Although the winery is only two miles from bustling downtown Sonoma, the quiet, forested grounds seem of another time. Carved antique wine casks are displayed near the original buildings, which are on both state and national registers of historic places. It was here that Buena Vista founder, Hungarian Count Agoston Haraszthy, helped introduce the prized European grapevine (*Vitus vinifera*) to California. Before then, the only wine grapes in Sonoma were Mission grapes planted and tended by the Franciscan friars who established Mission San Francisco de Solano on what is now Sonoma Plaza.

Haraszthy's life story would make a fascinating book or movie. A former member of the Hungarian Royal Guard, he immigrated in 1842 to Wisconsin, where he introduced sheep raising, was the first person to grow hops successfully, and operated the first ferryboat service on the Great Lakes. Asthma forced him to seek a milder climate, which led him in 1850 to San Diego. He then entered politics, rising as far as the state legislature. Despite all these accomplishments, Haraszthy had yet to realize his dream of growing wine grapes. After experimenting with European grapevines, he selected Sonoma for its ideal climate and in 1857 began planting his vineyards. Haraszthy hired Chinese laborers to dig long tunnels into the hillside as they built the Press House in 1862. This ivy-covered stone building now houses the tasting room; portions of two small caves can be viewed there. The house is also home to a gallery featuring the work of local artists who are available on the first weekend of each month to discuss their work and art in general.

After Haraszthy died at age fifty-six, Buena Vista closed temporarily beginning in 1879, but was revived in the 1940s by Frank Bartholomew. The winery's modern era dates to 1979, when the Moller-Racke family bought Buena Vista and invested in Carneros vineyard land before selling to the current owners. Today Buena Vista owns eleven hundred acres of land in Carneros, of which more than seven hundred are planted in vineyards.

CHATEAU SOUVERAIN WINERY

The imposing chateau perched on a knoll makes this winery one of the most impressive sights in Sonoma County. Approaching the estate beneath an arch connecting two tall stone pillars, visitors often feel a sense of occasion. The driveway, lined with gray-green olive trees, is surrounded by Zinfandel vines whose colors and textures change with the season, from bleak and gnarled in the dead of winter to a lush green canopy in spring and summer, to a palette of gold and orange as harvest approaches in the fall.

The twenty-five-acre grounds are a mixture of casual landscaping, including some 180 rosebushes, and the kind of formal gardens that befit a chateau. The buildings appear to consist almost entirely of steeply pitched slate-tile roofs, an impression that heightens the dramatic effect. A broad staircase leads from the parking lot to a gravel-lined courtyard where wooden benches face a square pool with a fountain in the  middle. Around the courtyard are small trees, roses, and lavender plants. Flowering vines climb the walls of the winery. The ambience is undeniably Mediterranean.

Chateau Souverain Winery was designed by architect John Marsh Davis and built in 1973. Blending the feel of a French chateau with elements of the historic Sonoma hop kilns that once proliferated in this part of the county, Davis constructed two prominent towers connected by a long, low-rise building that houses the wine cellar. One tower serves as the business offices. The other, the one guests see when they approach the winery, is home to the tasting room as well as the winery's restaurant. Davis's design won an American Institute of Architects Design Excellence Award in 1974.

The views from the courtyard and the tasting room encompass the estate vineyards in the foreground and the profile of 4,344-foot Mount St. Helena to the east. The most spectacular vistas are available from the outdoor tables at the café. This bistro-style restaurant specializes in regional fare such as fresh seafood, artisanal cheeses, free-range poultry, and organic produce. Chef Martin Courtman, who has been at the winery since 1991, honors local purveyors by listing their names on the back of the menu. Courtman has instituted a daily afternoon Sips and Temptations menu along the lines of an English tea service, with a three-tiered stand of small bites and flights of wine to match. The café's wines are from Chateau Souverain, which showcases the best grapes from the winery's estate vineyards, as well as from the top Sonoma County viticultural areas for each variety.

CHATEAU SOUVERAIN WINERY
400 Souverain Rd.
Geyserville, CA 95441
888-80-WINES
www.chateausouverain.com

OWNER: Beringer Blass Wine Estates.

LOCATION: About 5 miles north of Healdsburg via U.S. 101.

APPELLATION: Alexander Valley.

HOURS: 10 A.M.–5 P.M. daily.

TASTINGS: $5 (applied to wine purchase).

TOURS: None.

THE WINES: Cabernet Sauvignon, Chardonnay, Merlot, Sauvignon Blanc, Syrah, Zinfandel.

SPECIALTIES: Cabernet Sauvignon, Chardonnay.

WINEMAKER: Ed Killian.

ANNUAL PRODUCTION: 145,000 cases.

OF SPECIAL NOTE: Chateau Souverain Library Reserve Cabernet Sauvignon, Mourvedre, Syrah Port, Viognier, and Reserve Zinfandel available only at winery. Bottle limits on some small-production wines and reserve wines. Food and wine accessories, apparel, glassware, and books sold in winery shop. Two picnic areas; restaurant open for lunch daily and for dinner Friday–Sunday.

NEARBY ATTRACTIONS: Lake Sonoma (boating, camping, hiking).

CHATEAU ST. JEAN WINERY

CHATEAU ST. JEAN WINERY
8555 Hwy. 12
Kenwood, CA 95452
707-833-4134
www.chateaustjean.com

OWNER: Beringer Blass
Wine Estates.

LOCATION: 8 miles east of
Santa Rosa off U.S. 101.

APPELLATION: Sonoma
Valley.

HOURS: 10 A.M.–5 P.M. daily.

TASTINGS: $5 for 3 wines
in Tasting Room; $10 in
Reserve Tasting Room.

TOURS: By appointment.

THE WINES: Cabernet Franc,
Cabernet Sauvignon,
Chardonnay, Fumé Blanc,
Gewürztraminer,
Johannisberg Riesling,
Late-Harvest Johannisberg
Riesling, Merlot, Pinot
Blanc, Pinot Noir, Viognier.

SPECIALTIES: Single
vineyard–designated wines.

WINEMAKER: Steve Reeder.

ANNUAL PRODUCTION:
300,000 cases.

OF SPECIAL NOTE: Picnic
tables in oak-and-redwood
grove. Classes and seminars
on wine. Open houses on
most holidays. Large store
offering local cheeses,
meats, and breads, as well
as other merchandise.

NEARBY ATTRACTIONS:
Sugarloaf Ridge State
Park (hiking, camping,
horseback riding).

With the dramatic profile of Sugarloaf Ridge as a backdrop, the exquisitely landscaped grounds at Chateau St. Jean in Kenwood evoke the image of a grand country estate. The chateau itself dates to the 1920s, but it wasn't until 1973 that a family of Central Valley, California, growers of table grapes founded the winery. They named it after a favorite relative and, with tongue in cheek, placed a statue of "St. Jean" in the garden.

The winery building was constructed from the ground up to suit Chateau St. Jean's particular style of winemaking. The founders believed in the European practice of creating vineyard-designated wines, so they designed the winery to accommodate numerous lots of grapes, which could be kept separate throughout the winemaking process. Wines from each special vineyard are also bottled and marketed separately, with the vineyard name on the label. The winery produces eleven vineyard-designated wines from the Sonoma Valley, Alexander Valley, Russian River Valley, and Carneros appellations. The winery also makes other premium varietals and one famously successful blend. Chateau St. Jean became the first Sonoma winery to be awarded the prestigious "Wine of the Year" award from *Wine Spectator* magazine for its 1996 Cinq Cépages, a Bordeaux-style blend of five varieties.

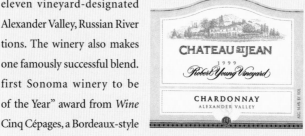

Noted winemaker Steve Reeder joined Chateau St. Jean in 1997, bringing nearly twenty years of winemaking experience—including a five-year tenure at Kendall-Jackson. His intimate knowledge of Sonoma's microclimates and his ability to bring out the best of each vineyard has furthered the winery's reputation as a pioneer of single vineyard–designated premium wines.

In the summer of 2000, Chateau St. Jean opened the doors to its new Visitor Center and Gardens. A formal Mediterranean-style garden contains roses, herbs, and citrus trees planted in oversized terra-cotta urns that are arranged to create a number of open-air "rooms." Picnickers have always been welcome to relax on the winery's redwood-studded grounds, but now the setting is enhanced by the extensive plantings, making the one-acre garden attractive throughout the year.

Beyond the Mediterranean garden is the new tasting room with a stunning, custom-made bar. Fashioned from mahogany with ebony accents, the thirty-five-foot-long bar is topped with sheet zinc. The elegant chateau now houses the Reserve Tasting Room. Visitors who would like to learn more about Chateau St. Jean wines are encouraged to attend the winery's educational seminars. Introductory classes are offered daily, while more in-depth programs are available by reservation.

CLINE CELLARS

CLINE CELLARS
24737 Hwy. 121
Sonoma, CA 95476
707-940-4000
800-546-2070
cbeltrano@clinecellars.com
www.clinecellars.com

OWNERS: Fred and Nancy Cline.

LOCATION: About 5 miles south of the town of Sonoma.

APPELLATION: Carneros.

HOURS: 10 A.M.–6 P.M. daily.

TASTINGS: Complimentary.

TOURS: 11 A.M., 1 P.M., and 3 P.M. daily.

THE WINES: Carignane, Marsanne, Mourvèdre, Pinot Gris, Syrah, Viognier, Zinfandel.

SPECIALTIES: Zinfandel and Rhône-style wines.

WINEMAKER: Charles Tsegeletos.

ANNUAL PRODUCTION: 220,000 cases.

OF SPECIAL NOTE: Look for turtles and fish in mineral pools built in the 1880s for raising carp. 130-year-old graffiti on old bathhouse wall. Cookbooks, deli items, and condiments sold in winery shop.

NEARBY ATTRACTIONS: Vintage Aircraft (scenic and aerobatic biplane rides); Infineon Raceway (auto racing); Train Town (rides for children).

Five thousand rosebushes stand shoulder to shoulder beside the low stone wall that winds its way onto the winery grounds. From April through December, they provide a riot of fragrant pink, white, red, and yellow blossoms. Picnic tables are scattered around the lawn, shaded by magnolias and other trees. Weeping willows hover over the mineral pools on either side of the restored 1850s farmhouse where the tasting room is located. The white farmhouse is rimmed with a picturesque dark green porch set with small wrought-iron tables and chairs where visitors can sip wine at their leisure.

Cline Cellars was originally established in Oakley, California, some forty miles east of San Francisco. Founder Fred Cline had spent his childhood summers learning farming and winemaking from his grandfather, Valeriano Jacuzzi (of spa and pump fame). Cline started the winery in 1982 with a $12,000 inheritance from the sale of Jacuzzi Bros. Four years later, his brother Matt joined Cline Cellars as the winemaker  after studying viticulture at the University of California at Davis. In 1991, the Cline Cellars facilities were relocated to this 350-acre estate in the Carneros District at the southern end of the Sonoma Valley.

The Cline estate occupies a historical parcel of land first settled by the Miwok Indians. Nearby, a nineteenth-century bathhouse harks to the time when the white settlers realized something that the Miwoks had known all along: warm mineral baths are good for you. While the town of Sonoma is generally considered the original site of the Sonoma mission, the mission was actually founded here when Father Altimira installed a cross on July 4, 1823. Perhaps it was the constant Carneros breezes that inspired him to pull up stakes and relocate to the town of Sonoma later that same year.

The Clines specialize in Zinfandel and Rhône varietals. Their Ancient Vines Carignane, Zinfandel, and Mourvèdre wines are produced from some of the oldest and rarest vines in the state. The Mourvèdre grapevines represent approximately 85 percent of California's total supply of this versatile varietal. The Sonoma location was selected especially for its relatively cool climate; chilly fog and frequent strong afternoon winds mitigate the summertime heat that blisters the rest of the Sonoma Valley. When the Clines bought the property, they planted all-new vineyards of Rhône varietals such as Syrah, Viognier, Marsanne, and Roussanne.

DAVIS BYNUM WINERY

DAVIS BYNUM WINERY
8075 Westside Rd.
Healdsburg, CA 95448
707-433-2611
800-826-1073
info@davisbynum.com
www.davisbynum.com

OWNER: Davis Bynum.

LOCATION: 8 miles west of Healdsburg.

APPELLATION: Russian River Valley.

HOURS: 10 A.M.–5 P.M. daily.

TASTINGS: Complimentary except for very limited lots.

TOURS: None of winery.

THE WINES: Cabernet Sauvignon, Chardonnay, Fumé Blanc, Meritage, Merlot, Pinot Noir, Zinfandel.

SPECIALTY: Lindley's Knoll Estate Grown Pinot Noir.

WINEMAKER: David Georges.

ANNUAL PRODUCTION: 12,200 cases.

OF SPECIAL NOTE: Tours of permaculture garden available to groups of 10–25 by reservation and on designated weekends such as annual mid-August Grapes to Glass event. Three-bottle limit on some Pinot Noirs.

NEARBY ATTRACTIONS: Armstrong Redwoods State Reserve (hiking, horseback riding, picnic facilities); Russian River (swimming, canoe and kayak rentals).

Davis Bynum made history in 1973 when he set up shop in an abandoned hop kiln and established the first winery on the Russian River Valley's Westside Road. It wasn't until ten years later that the valley was officially recognized as an American Viticultural Area (AVA), or appellation, by the U.S. Bureau of Alcohol, Tobacco and Firearms. The winding, tree-shaded road is home to at least a dozen other grape growers and winemakers who have come to appreciate the agricultural attributes of this western Sonoma valley.

Davis Bynum had inherited a love of wine from his father, an amateur winemaker, just as his son Hampton, now general manager, inherited it from Davis. Davis began experimenting with home winemaking in the 1950s, and the hobby grew into a business when he transformed a Berkeley warehouse into a winery. In 1973, he graduated into the big leagues when he bought the eighty-four-acre River Bend Ranch in western Sonoma. The ranch's hop kiln, where locally grown hops were once processed into beer, was built in 1950 but had fallen into disuse in 1953. Today it houses the winery and tasting room. Next to the kiln is an old barn that is graced each spring with a spectacular display of lavender wisteria.

DAVIS BYNUM
2000
RUSSIAN RIVER VALLEY
PINOT NOIR
ALC.13.9% BY VOL.

Located less than twenty miles from the Pacific Ocean, Davis Bynum Winery cultivates twenty-two acres of its own ranch property. All the grapevines—Pinot Noir, Merlot, Cabernet Sauvignon, and Chardonnay—are organically farmed. The pastoral Russian River Valley is known for its extremely cool growing conditions, which allow the grapes to ripen slowly over an extended period. As a result, they have sufficient time to develop intense varietal fruit character balanced with natural acidity. Since 1995, Davis Bynum has reduced the winery's annual output from thirty thousand cases to just over twelve thousand. Believing that producing less wine allows for more attention to quality, the family—including Davis, Hampton, and Hampton's sister, Susan—decided to focus on its strengths: location and longtime relationships with quality grape suppliers.

Concerned about the monoculture of grape growing, the family established a 3.5-acre permaculture garden adjacent to their vineyards. As defined by Bill Mollison, co-founder of the concept, the purpose is to create "agriculturally productive ecosystems which have the diversity, stability, and resilience of natural ecosystems." Plants were chosen for their usefulness and sustainability, and the land was shaped to recharge the groundwater and prevent erosion. Roses, grapes, mulberry trees, and flowering vines provide a habitat for beneficial insects that help deter pests such as sharpshooters, which are harmful to grapes. Owls, hawks, and bald eagles find refuge here as well.

GLORIA FERRER CHAMPAGNE CAVES

GLORIA FERRER CHAMPAGNE CAVES
23555 Hwy. 121
Sonoma, CA 95476
707-996-7256
info@gloriaferrer.com
www.gloriaferrer.com

OWNER: Freixenet, S.A.

LOCATION: 6 miles south of town of Sonoma.

APPELLATION: Carneros.

HOURS: 10:30 A.M.–5:30 P.M. daily.

TASTINGS: $4–7 per glass of sparkling wine; $1–3 for table wine.

TOURS: Daily during hours of operation.

THE WINES: Blanc de Noirs, Brut, Brut Rosé, Chardonnay, Merlot, Pinot Noir, Syrah.

SPECIALTIES: Brut Rosé, José S. Ferrer Reserve, Carneros Cuvée ETS.

WINEMAKER: Bob Iantosca.

ANNUAL PRODUCTION: 100,000 cases.

OF SPECIAL NOTE: Spanish cookbooks and locally made products, as well as deli items, sold at the winery. Annual Catalan Festival (July).

NEARBY ATTRACTIONS: Mission San Francisco Solano and other historic buildings in downtown Sonoma; Vintage Aircraft (scenic and aerobatic biplane rides); Infineon Raceway (auto racing); Viansa Winery Wetlands (tours).

The Carneros District, with its continual winds and cool marine air, is known far and wide as an ideal climate for growing Pinot Noir and Chardonnay grapes. The word spread all the way to Spain, where the Ferrer family had been making sparkling wine for more than a century. In 1889, Pedro Ferrer founded Freixenet, now one of the world's two largest producers of sparkling wine.

Members of the family had been looking for vineyard land in the United States off and on for fifty years when José and Gloria Ferrer visited the southern part of the Sonoma Valley. The climate reminded them of their Catalan home in Spain, and in 1982, they acquired a forty-acre pasture and then, four years later, another two hundred acres nearby. They started planting vineyards with Pinot Noir and Chardonnay, the traditional sparkling wine grapes. In addition to sparkling wines, Gloria Ferrer produces still wines, including Merlot, Pinot Noir, and Chardonnay.

The wines have a history of critical success. Within a year of its 1986 debut, the winery won seven gold medals and a Sweepstakes Award at the San Francisco Fair's International Wine Competition.

The winery that José Ferrer built was the first champagne facility in the Carneros. Named for his wife, it was designed after a *masia* (a Catalan farmhouse), complete with terraces, a red tile roof, and thick walls the color of the Spanish plains. Complementing the exterior, the winery's cool interior has dark tile floors and Spanish textiles. The ties to Spain continue in the winery's shop, which offers a selection of cookbooks devoted to Spanish cuisine and the specialties of Catalonia. Also available are Sonoma-grown products such as Gloria Ferrer's champagne and Chardonnay-jalapeño mustards, white truffle–grapeseed oil, and champagne-filled chocolates.

Visitors are welcome to enjoy their wines, both still and sparkling, in the spacious tasting room—where a fire roars in the fireplace on winter days—or outside on the Vista Terrace. There they are treated to a breathtaking view of the Carneros District and the upper reaches of San Pablo Bay. On a clear day, they can see all the way to the peak of Mt. Diablo in the East Bay. Both still and sparkling wines are aged in the caves tunneled into the hill behind the hospitality center. Winery tours include a visit to these aromatic dark recesses where guides explain the traditional *méthode champenoise* process of creating sparkling wine, during which the wine undergoes its secondary fermentation—the one that forms the characteristic bubbles—in the bottle, not in the barrel.

IMAGERY ESTATE WINERY

When is a wine bottle more than just a wine bottle? When it is adorned with an original work of art. This is the case for the wines in the Imagery Estate Winery's Artist Collection, each bottle of which has a distinctive label bearing artwork. The contemporary artists commissioned to create the labels include Robert Arneson, Chester Arnold, Squeak Carnwath, Roy De Forest, Mary Frank, David Gilhooly, David Nash, Nathan Oliveira, William Wiley, and Chihung Yang. The winery itself is almost as much a gallery as it is a winemaking facility and even has its own curator, Bob Nugent, a recognized artist with strong ties to the national art community. Nugent has organized the 125 pieces of original label art into a permanent display in the hospitality center. Like the winemaking facility behind it, the hospitality center is in an off-white modern building that is surprisingly compatible with the bucolic Sonoma Valley.

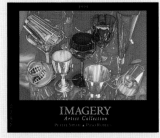

The most important artist at the winery, however, is Joe Benziger. A member of the acclaimed family that runs the nearby Benziger Family Winery, Joe Benziger has been the creative force behind the Imagery wines since their inception. He handles every detail of the winery's two tiers, the Artist Collection and the Vineyard Collection. The Artist Collection is known for its limited quantities of uncommon varietal offerings, such as Petite Sirah and Malbec. The newer Vineyard Collection features only select, single-vineyard wines from exceptional vineyards throughout Sonoma, Napa, and North Coast appellations.

The original Artist Collection dates to 1985, when the owners of Benziger Family Winery and Imagery Estate Winery found themselves with two small lots of exceptional Chardonnay and Zinfandel. The challenge was to find a way to showcase wines that were too limited to market nationally but too special to ignore. As serendipity would have it, winemaker Joe Benziger happened to meet Bob Nugent at a local polo match. That encounter led to Nugent's creation of a wine label. By the second vintage, the concept evolved as a way to focus on esoteric grape varietals not readily available in most winery offerings.

The Imagery Estate wines became so popular that in the summer of 2000, the family moved the entire operation, including the winemaking facilities and the artwork, to their property on Highway 12, less than two miles from the Benziger Family Winery. This is where visitors now come to taste the wines and linger to admire the art collection, the largest of its kind in the United States.

IMAGERY ESTATE WINERY
14335 Hwy. 12
Glen Ellen, CA 95442
707-935-4515
877-550-4278
info@imagerywinery.com
www.imagerywinery.com

OWNERS: Benziger family.

LOCATION: 3 miles north of the town of Sonoma via Hwy. 12.

APPELLATION: Sonoma Valley.

HOURS: 10 A.M.–4:30 P.M. daily.

TASTINGS: $5 for 5 wines.

TOURS: None.

THE WINES: Barbera, Cabernet Franc, Cabernet Sauvignon, Chardonnay, Malbec, Petite Sirah, Pinot Blanc, Sangiovese, Viognier, White Burgundy.

SPECIALTIES: Limited-production varietals.

WINEMAKER: Joe Benziger.

ANNUAL PRODUCTION: 5,000 cases.

OF SPECIAL NOTE: Most wines available only in tasting room. Gallery of 125 original artworks commissioned by winery; patio seating; picnic area; bocce ball court. Limited-edition wine-label posters and extensive collection of serving pieces at winery shop.

NEARBY ATTRACTIONS: Jack London State Historic Park (museum, hiking, horseback riding); Sonoma Valley Regional Park (hiking, dog park).

J VINEYARDS AND WINERY

J VINEYARDS AND WINERY
11447 Old Redwood Hwy.
Healdsburg, CA 95448
707-431-3646
winefolk@jwine.com
www.jwine.com

OWNER: Judy Jordan.

LOCATION: About 3 miles south of Healdsburg.

APPELLATION: Russian River Valley.

HOURS: 11 A.M.–5 P.M. daily.

TASTINGS: $5–15 for 1–5 wines.

TOURS: By appointment.

THE WINES: Brut, Chardonnay, Pinotage, Pinot Gris, Pinot Noir, Viognier.

SPECIALTIES: Pinot Noir, sparkling wine.

WINEMAKER: Oded Shakked.

ANNUAL PRODUCTION: 50,000 cases.

OF SPECIAL NOTE: Pinotage, Robert Thomas Vineyards Pinot Noir, and Viognier available only at winery.

NEARBY ATTRACTIONS: Russian River (swimming, canoe and kayak rentals); hot-air balloon rides from winery parking lot.

Winery owner Judy Jordan has lived on a commune in China, trekked the Sahara by camel, toured Romania with former KGB members, and worked on a ranch in the Australian outback. An experienced geologist with a prestigious degree from Stanford University, Jordan rose to the position of vice president in charge of operations at her father's Healdsburg winery, Jordan Vineyard and Winery. While still working at Jordan, she formed a partnership with her father, Tom, to launch J Vineyards and Winery in 1986. Jordan, who is also a wife and mother, might be described as an overachiever. She brought that same drive for perfection, along with a commitment to innovation, to her own winery, and it shows in the details, right down to the wine labels. For instance,  the distinctive golden *J* adorning each bottle stands for Judy and also honors her family name.

The most notable innovation at the winery is the food-and-wine-pairing program. Many Northern California wineries adhere to the concept that wine should be enjoyed with food, but the only food served in most tasting rooms is a bowl of wafers. At J Vineyards, wines are always accompanied by fine food, elegant morsels that have been selected and specifically prepared by the winery's professional chef and culinary staff to complement a particular wine. The selections, which change with the seasons, might include foie gras or eggplant caviar served with sparkling wine, smoked salmon tartare or curried shrimp with Pinot Gris, local cheese with Chardonnay, or duck rillettes with Pinot Noir.

These pairings are conducted at a long bar that extends across the back of the spacious tasting room. Behind it is an enormous, eye-catching wall in which bubbles appear to be rising. This work of art in jagged glass and fiber optics was designed by Gordon Huether, now the artist-in-residence at Artesa Winery in Napa. Majolica ceramics from Italy, crystal trifle bowls and cake plates from Poland, and a selection of fine linens are more than merely retail items; they also complement Huether's vision.

Founding a winery is one thing, but finding a winery is another. Jordan Sparkling Wine Company, as it was originally known, made its first vintage, J Sparkling Wine, in 1987 using the facilities at Jordan Winery, but it would be another nine years before the company had a home of its own. In 1996, the winery acquired the former Piper Sonoma facility and, after extensive remodeling, opened for business as J Vineyards and Winery three years later.

KENWOOD VINEYARDS

The photogenic, century-old barn where visitors come to taste Kenwood's wines dates to one of the most romantic eras in Sonoma Valley history. The quintessential adventure author Jack London was living, writing, and raising grapes in nearby Glen Ellen when the Pagani Brothers established their winery in 1906 in the buildings that now house Kenwood Vineyards. In those days, long before the invention of tasting rooms, wine lovers would bring their own barrels and jugs to be filled and then cart them home.

Decades later, in 1970, a trio of wine enthusiasts from the San Francisco Bay Area founded Kenwood Vineyards. In redesigning and modernizing the existing winery, they created a facility that allows the winemaker the utmost in flexibility. More than 125 stainless steel fermenting and upright oak tanks are utilized in combination with some 17,000 French and American oak barrels. Kenwood uses estate fruit as well as grapes from some of Sonoma County's best vineyards and follows the *cuvée* winemaking method, in which the harvest from each vineyard is handled separately to preserve its individual character. According to winemaker Michael Lee, one of the winery's founders, such "small lot" winemaking allows each lot of grapes to be brought to its fullest potential before blending. Likewise, the acclaimed Artist Series is a masterful blend of the top barrels of Cabernet Sauvignon.

The historic barn and other original buildings lend a nostalgic ambience to the modern winemaking facilities on the twenty-two-acre estate. But there is another link to the romantic history of the Valley of the Moon, as author London dubbed Sonoma Valley.

Best known for his rugged individualism and dynamic writing, London was also an accomplished farmer and rancher. At the heart of his Beauty Ranch—now part of the Jack London State Historic Park—several hundred acres of vineyards were planted in the 1870s on terraced slopes. The volcanic ash fields produced excellent wines by the turn of the twentieth century. London died in 1916, and by World War II, his crop fields had become overgrown. But in 1976, Kenwood Vineyards became the exclusive marketer of wines produced from the ranch. The Cabernet Sauvignon, Zinfandel, Merlot, and Pinot Noir, made only from Jack London vineyard grapes, bear a label with the image of a wolf's head, London's signature stamp.

Known for consistency of quality in both its red and its white wines, Kenwood produces mostly moderately priced wines. The major exception is the Artist Series Cabernet Sauvignons, which have been collector's items since first released in 1978.

KENWOOD VINEYARDS
9592 Hwy. 12
Kenwood, CA 95452
707-833-5891
info@heckestates.com
www.kenwoodvineyards.com

OWNER: F. Korbel & Bros.

LOCATION: 15 miles southeast of Santa Rosa on Hwy. 12.

APPELLATION: Sonoma Valley.

HOURS: 10 A.M.–4:30 P.M. daily.

TASTINGS: Complimentary; $5 for Private Reserve wines.

TOURS: 11:30 A.M. and 2:30 P.M. daily, except during special events. Reservations required for groups of 8 or more.

THE WINES: Cabernet Sauvignon, Chardonnay, Gewürztraminer, Merlot, Pinot Noir, Sauvignon Blanc, sparkling wines, White Zinfandel, Zinfandel.

SPECIALTIES: Artist Series, Jack London Ranch wines.

WINEMAKER: Michael Lee.

ANNUAL PRODUCTION: 550,000 cases.

OF SPECIAL NOTE: Monthly themed food-and-wine events matching chef's specialties with appropriate wines. Limited-release Artist Series wines available only at winery.

NEARBY ATTRACTIONS: Jack London State Historic Park (museum, hiking, horseback riding); Sugarloaf Ridge State Park (hiking, camping, horseback riding).

LANDMARK VINEYARDS

LANDMARK VINEYARDS
101 Adobe Canyon Rd.
Kenwood, CA 95452
707-833-0053
info@landmarkwine.com
www.landmarkwine.com

OWNERS: Mary and Michael Colhoun.

LOCATION: 11.5 miles north of town of Sonoma off Hwy. 12.

APPELLATION: Sonoma Valley.

HOURS: 10 A.M.–4:30 P.M. daily.

TASTINGS: Complimentary.

TOURS: By appointment.

THE WINES: Chardonnay, Pinot Noir.

SPECIALTY: Handcrafted wines fermented with wild yeast.

WINEMAKER: Eric Stern.

ANNUAL PRODUCTION: 25,000 cases.

OF SPECIAL NOTE: Pondside picnic area; bocce ball court; horse-drawn wagon rides in vineyards (summer weekends only). Range of picnic baskets and wine-related accessories at winery shop.

NEARBY ATTRACTIONS: Sugarloaf State Park (hiking, camping, horseback riding); Annadel State Park (hiking, biking).

The low-rise California mission–style architecture of Landmark Vineyards looks so appropriate to the site that the buildings might have been there for a century. This family-owned winery was actually built in 1987, when founder Damaris Deere Ethridge decided to relocate her winery in northwestern Sonoma County to this twenty-acre estate in the heart of the Sonoma Valley. The elegant complex surrounded by vineyards is graced with abundant natural light and expansive views of the forested slopes of Sugarloaf Mountain. A brick walkway lined with rosebushes leads from the entrance into a courtyard showcasing a low blue-tiled fountain that sends a spray of water nearly twenty feet. Around the fountain are six Italian cypress, planted in a semicircle.

One element that might seem curious to first-time visitors is the bright green, 1946 John Deere tractor displayed near the entrance to the winery. But this is a very fitting artifact, since founder Damaris Ethridge is a direct descendant of John Deere, who invented the steel plow in 1838 and thus changed the American agricultural landscape forever. The family's commitment to innovation and respect for the land remains evident today in its approach to winemaking.

Michael Deere Colhoun, who owns the winery with his wife, Mary T. Colhoun, is credited with the vision and talent that transformed what was once a little-known winery into one of the most heralded producers of Chardonnay and Pinot Noir in California. While many wineries make a wide range of wines, Landmark decided to specialize in these two Burgundian varietals, fully aware that the Pinot Noir grape is among the most fickle in the world. Key to their success is the careful selection of vineyards, each of which is chosen for the ability of its grapes to produce stellar wine. Equally important is the use of wild yeasts contained in the waxy coating, or bloom, of the grape skin, as well as yeasts that occur naturally in the local environment, in place of factory-produced yeasts. When the grape juice is transferred into French oak barrels, the wild yeasts not only transform the juice into wine, but also create a wide array of secondary compounds that lend the wines great depth and complexity. The incorporation of these naturally occurring yeasts is integral to the traditional Burgundian style of winemaking.

The centerpiece of the Landmark tasting room is a dramatic mural painted on canvas by noted Sonoma County artist Claudia Wagar. Hovering between impressionism and realism, the imagery unfolds from foreground to background—from a close-up of a grape cluster against grapevines in neat rows to the rolling green hills of Sonoma Valley and Sugarloaf Mountain in the background.

LEDSON WINERY AND VINEYARDS

Locals call it "the castle"—the Gothic edifice that took ten years and some 2 million bricks to create. As they drove up and down the highway in front of it, they wondered if it was a house or an elegant winery. When the Ledson family started construction in 1989, they thought the property would be ideal for their residence. They planted Merlot and Zinfandel vineyards and began work on the house. As the months passed, the turrets, slate roofs, balconies, and fountains took shape, and passersby would even climb over the fences to get a better look.

Steve Ledson finally realized it was time to rethink his plan. Given the intense public interest in the building and the quality of his grape harvests—which he sold to nearby wineries—he decided to turn the sixteen-thousand-square-foot structure into a winery and tasting room. In 1997, he released the winery's first wine: the 1994 Estate Merlot. After two years of reconstruction, the winery opened in 1999.

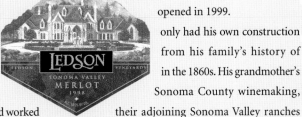

Fortunately, Ledson not only had his own construction company but also benefited from his family's history of farming in the area, beginning in the 1860s. His grandmother's father was an early pioneer in Sonoma County winemaking, and both sets of grandparents had worked their adjoining Sonoma Valley ranches cooperatively. Eventually, this Ledson acreage became part of Annadel State Park. Steve Ledson, the fourth generation to farm in the area, had always wanted to grow grapes, and when he had the chance, he bought the twenty-one-acre property—which just happened to have a view of Annadel park.

Visitors to the castle today find an estate worthy of the French countryside, with a grand brick driveway, a manicured landscape, and a flourishing collection of roses. Just inside the front door is a huge curved staircase and three spacious rooms for tasting and shopping. The curious will delight in finding remnants of the original architecture, such as mini-Gothic fireplaces in the retail shop. The interior was designed entirely by Steve Ledson and features ornate wood inlays and mosaics created by son Mike.

The Marketplace at Ledson proffers an impressive selection of international gourmet products, including more than a hundred cheeses from around the world and premium meats, as well as imported and local olive oils. Also featured are freshly baked breads, homemade salads, fresh local produce, and sandwiches. Guests are encouraged to create their own wine country picnic for enjoying in the century-old oak grove next to the vineyard or alongside the fountain. Then, they have only to cross the street to hike the miles of trails in Annadel State Park.

LEDSON WINERY AND VINEYARDS
7335 Hwy. 12
Kenwood, CA 95452
707-833-2330
hospitality@ledson.com
www.ledson.com

OWNER:
Steve Noble Ledson.

LOCATION: About 2 mi. northwest of Kenwood.

APPELLATION:
Sonoma Valley.

HOURS: 10 A.M.–5 P.M. daily.

TASTINGS: $5 for 5 wines; $10 for 3 reserve and library wines.

TOURS: None.

THE WINES: Barbera, Chardonnay, Dolcetto, Gewürztraminer, Johannisberg Riesling, Merlot, Orange Muscat, Pinot Noir, Sangiovese, Sauvignon Blanc, Zinfandel.

SPECIALTY: Merlot.

WINEMAKER:
Steve Noble Ledson.

ANNUAL PRODUCTION:
20,000 cases.

OF SPECIAL NOTE: Ledson wines available only at winery and at fine restaurants. Wine-tasting events held at least once a month. Extensive selection of gourmet products and picnic foods at Marketplace.

NEARBY ATTRACTIONS:
Sugarloaf State Park (hiking, camping, horseback riding); Annadel State Park (hiking, biking).

MATANZAS CREEK WINERY AND ESTATE GARDENS

MATANZAS CREEK WINERY AND ESTATE GARDENS
6097 Bennett Valley Rd.
Santa Rosa, CA 95404
800-590-6464
info@matanzascreek.com
www.matanzascreek.com

OWNERS: Jess Jackson and
Barbara Banke.

LOCATION: About 6 miles
southeast of Santa Rosa
via Bennett Valley Rd.

APPELLATION: Sonoma
Valley.

HOURS: 10 A.M.–4:30 P.M.
daily, April–December;
closed Monday, Tuesday,
and Wednesday, January–
March.

TASTINGS: $5 for 8 tastes.

TOURS: 10:30 A.M. and
3 P.M., Monday–Friday, by
appointment only. Self-
guided tours of garden
during operating hours.

THE WINES: Cabernet
Sauvignon, Chardonnay,
Merlot, Sauvignon Blanc,
Syrah.

SPECIALTIES: Chardonnay,
Merlot.

WINEMAKER: Even Bakke.

ANNUAL PRODUCTION:
40,000–45,000 cases.

OF SPECIAL NOTE: Picnic
area beneath oak trees
with vineyard views. Gift
shop featuring soap,
sachets, grilling sticks, and
other items made from
winery's lavender.

NEARBY ATTRACTIONS:
Luther Burbank Garden
and Home (tours of famed
horticulturist's property).

Beside a scenic stretch of rural Bennett Valley Road, eye-catching fields of lavender create an image evocative of Provence. In spring and summer, their heady fragrance wafts over the winery property, cloaking the old oak trees in an invisible mist. Throughout the year, lavender stems and blossoms provide the Matanzas Creek Winery gift shop with a bounty of handcrafted soaps, lotions, and other products. It's not likely the supply will run out anytime soon: the winery's estimated forty-five-hundred plants yield more than 2 million stems, enough to keep the winery in production all year. The crop is the largest of its kind in Northern California.

As beautiful as the lavender fields are, they cover only 2 acres of the 219-acre Bennett Valley estate, which was assembled  piece by piece by founder Sandra (Stern) MacIver. The daughter of a prominent New Orleans family with no knowledge of the wine industry, she nonetheless set out to establish her own winery. She bought the first 100 acres in 1971 at an estate liquidation sale, including some dilapidated buildings from the original dairy farm but not much else. After the land was prepared, the first grapes, Chardonnay and Merlot, were planted on 22 acres in 1975. The following year, MacIver purchased an additional 119 adjacent acres and completed her first harvest. She established Matanzas Creek Winery in 1977 in a converted milking shed.

In 1978, Sandra met Bill MacIver, a retired U.S. Air Force captain, who would become her partner in business as well as marriage. Together, they forged a company that quickly gained notice when their 1979 Chardonnay won the coveted Sweepstakes Award at the prestigious Sonoma County Harvest Fair in 1981. In 1984, production having overwhelmed the small winery, they began building a new winemaking facility, which opened in 1985.

It wasn't until 1991 that the MacIvers found time to establish the extensive gardens that are now such an integral part of any visit to the winery. In addition to the lavender, visitors find billowing native grasses, olive trees with their slender, gray-green leaves, a variety of perennials, and, of course, the rows of grapevines in the distance. The gardens were inspired by those at the New Orleans home of Sandra MacIver's grandparents. In spring and summer, amateur and professional artists can often be seen painting in the fields, becoming part of the landscape themselves. Over the years, the MacIvers began exploring interests beyond the winery. In March of 2000, they sold Matanzas Creek to their close friends, Jess Jackson and Barbara Banke. The new owners have extensive winery experience as the proprietors of the world-famous Kendall-Jackson wine company.

MAZZOCCO VINEYARDS

Some people choose to give up in the face of disappointment, but not Tom Mazzocco. He was an ophthalmologist back in 1973 when he made his first batch of homemade wine and all five gallons of it ended up spattered on the floor, walls, and ceiling of a spare bathroom, thanks to a broken piece of equipment. Despite the initial setback, Mazzocco persevered with his home winemaking efforts. His reward came in 1980: he and his wife, Yvonne, purchased the River Lane Vineyard in Sonoma County's Alexander Valley. Their dream of making their own commercial wine came true the following year.

Inspired by that success, the Mazzoccos built their own winery on the west side of Highway 101 adjacent to the Healdsburg Municipal Airport. There they crushed their first Dry Creek Valley grapes in 1985. Now, with grapes from the original River Lane Vineyard—plus two estate vineyards in the Dry Creek Valley and others sourced from some of the county's top growers— the Mazzoccos produce nearly twenty thousand cases of wine annually.

They do this at a facility poised on a windswept ridge top with views to the east, west, and south. The exterior of the brown wood building looks like a postmodern barn, but the sleek interior has floor-to-ceiling glass walls on two sides, slate tiles from India on the floor, and a tasting bar made of black granite. From time to time, visitors are treated to the exhilarating sight of private planes taking off from the small airport. The airport proved handy when the Mazzoccos were constructing the winery and during its first few years. Until his retirement, Tom headed an eye-care center in Los Angeles and flew his own plane between Healdsburg and his practice.

Outside the tasting room are the vineyards from which Mazzocco makes many of its wines. Considering the limited production, it is impressive that the winery produces five Zinfandels and four vineyard-designated wines from Dry Creek Valley and one from Alexander Valley. Dry Creek Valley's warm, dry climate is considered ideal for a number of varietals, particularly Zinfandel, which typically expresses the flavors of a particular vineyard. The tasting room is a great place to learn to distinguish among Zinfandels from different vineyards, even those adjacent to one another.

MAZZOCCO VINEYARDS
1400 Lytton Springs Rd.
Healdsburg, CA 95448
707-431-8159
vino@mazzocco.com
www.mazzocco.com

OWNERS: Tom and Yvonne Mazzocco.

LOCATION: 1.5 miles west of Lytton Springs exit off U.S. 101 north.

APPELLATION: Dry Creek Valley.

HOURS: 10 A.M.–4:30 P.M. daily.

TASTINGS: Complimentary for 4 wines; $2 per glass for library wines.

TOURS: None.

THE WINES: Cabernet Sauvignon, Chardonnay, Matrix (a Bordeaux blend), Merlot, Sauvignon Blanc, Viognier, Zinfandel.

SPECIALTIES: Chardonnay, Zinfandel.

ANNUAL PRODUCTION: 17,000 cases.

OF SPECIAL NOTE: Annual events include Winter Wineland (January), Barrel Tasting (March), Passport to Dry Creek Valley (April), and Thanksgiving Open House (November). Tapestry pillows and scarves sold at winery shop.

NEARBY ATTRACTIONS: Russian River (swimming, canoe and kayak rentals); Lake Sonoma (boating, camping, hiking).

RAVENSWOOD WINERY

RAVENSWOOD WINERY
18701 Gehricke Rd.
Sonoma, CA 95476
707-938-1960
888-669-4679
rwwine@ravenswood-wine.com
www.ravenswood-wine.com

OWNER: Franciscan Estates, Fine Wine Division of Constellation Brands.

LOCATION: About .5 mile northeast of town of Sonoma via Fourth St. East and Lovall Valley Rd.

APPELLATION: Sonoma Valley.

HOURS: 10 A.M.–4:30 P.M. daily.

TASTINGS: $4 for 4 or 5 wines.

TOURS: By reservation; 10:30 A.M. daily.

THE WINES: Bordeaux-style blends, Cabernet Franc, Cabernet Sauvignon, Chardonnay, ICON (Rhone-style blend), Merlot, Petite Sirah, Zinfandel.

SPECIALTY: Zinfandel.

WINEMAKER: Joel Peterson.

ANNUAL PRODUCTION: 400,000 cases.

OF SPECIAL NOTE: Bicyclists and other visitors are welcome to picnic on stone patio with view of vineyards.

NEARBY ATTRACTIONS: Mission San Francisco Solano and other historic buildings in downtown Sonoma; bike rentals; Vella Cheese Company; Sonoma Cheese Factory; Train Town (rides for children).

Few wineries set out to make cult wines, and probably fewer, to produce more than 400,000 cases a year. Ravenswood has done both. Its founders began by crushing enough juice to make 327 cases of Zinfandel in 1976, and although the winery also makes other wines, Zinfandel remains king. Nearly three-quarters of Ravenswood's production is Zinfandel.

Winemaker and cofounder Joel Peterson and chairman and cofounder Reed Foster were so successful with that first, handcrafted vintage that they have had to live up to the standard it set ever since. Ravenswood produces fourteen different Zinfandels that represent the spectrum of the varietal's personality, with tastes ranging from peppery and spicy to chocolaty and minty. If there is one common denominator, it is reflected in the slogan adopted by the winery in 1990: "No Wimpy Wines."

Most of Ravenswood's grapes come from more than a hundred independent growers. It is those long-standing relationships that ensure the consistency of the wines. One vineyard source dates to 1986. The Strotz family invited Joel Peterson to visit their Sonoma Mountain vineyard, which they had named Pickberry because of all the wild blackberries harvested there. Peterson immediately recognized the quality of the Strotz grapes, and in 1988, Ravenswood released the first of its many blends of Cabernet Sauvignon, Cabernet Franc, and Merlot under the vineyard-designated name Pickberry.

Peterson never set out to specialize in Zinfandel; originally he was more interested in the Bordeaux varietals he began tasting at the age of ten with his father, Walter, founder of the San Francisco Wine Sampling Club. In time, however, he fell under the spell of Zinfandel. In the 1970s, after a brief career as a wine writer and consultant, he went to work for the late Joseph Swan, considered one of California's outstanding craftsmen of fine Zinfandel. Thus the stage was set for the varietal's ascendancy at the winery Peterson founded.

Ravenswood farms fourteen acres of estate vineyards on the northeast side of Sonoma. The old stone building, once home to the Haywood Winery, has extensive patio seating with beautiful south-facing views of the vineyards. Thanks to the company's growth, the winemaking operations have since been relocated to a forty-five-thousand-square-foot facility in the Carneros District, but the tasting room remains. Originally a cozy, even cramped affair, it was greatly expanded in 1996, and now has plenty of elbow room as well as ample natural light to sample and appreciate the wines.

RAYMOND BURR VINEYARDS

I n 1986, some thirty years after the hit television show "Perry Mason" made Raymond Burr a household name, the actor decided to follow another passion: making great wine. The small Dry Creek Valley estate that bears his name does not produce enough grapes to find the world-wide audience of a hit TV series, but its reputation is growing.

Burr met fellow actor Robert Benevides on the set of "Perry Mason," and they soon discovered that they shared an interest in appreciating wine and growing orchids. Eventually, the two friends turned both hobbies into viable commercial operations. In 1976, Benevides purchased forty prime acres of benchland at the foot of Bradford Mountain west of Healdsburg. As Burr's series "Ironside" was ending its eight-year run, the actor got his first look at the ranch. He must have been pleased: the view from the east-facing slopes of the property takes in a scenic swath of country-side, with hills and manzanita trees as far as the eye can see. In 1980, they relocated the commercial orchid nursery established several years earlier to the ranch and began developing the property.

The intimate, bungalow-style tasting room is filled with memorabilia from Raymond Burr's acting career, notably his Emmy awards and vintage issues of *TV Guide* with his picture on the covers. The space is cozy, so unless the weather is dismal, visitors take their glasses out to the patio, where they can be served in the shade of an old oak tree and take in the sweeping views. Sensational orchids can be seen in the greenhouses year-round, but fall is peak bloom season.

CABERNET SAUVIGNON
DRY CREEK VALLEY
1 9 9 9
ALC. 13.8% BY VOL.

The sixteen-acre vineyard is on a steeply terraced hillside with very well-drained soil, ideal conditions for premium Cabernet Sauvignon grapes. Although the Dry Creek Valley is a warm growing region, the east-facing vineyards are bathed in shade late in the day, and the cool air from the nearby ocean keeps the temperatures low at night. The combination allows the grapes to mature at a steady pace. The longer the fruit hangs on the vine, the more flavor it develops. As John Quinones, who joined Raymond Burr Vineyards as winemaker in 1998, says, "A winemaker can't create quality. It's our job to preserve and enhance what comes out of the vineyard." Currently the vineyard includes nine acres of Cabernet Sauvignon, five acres of Chardonnay, and two acres of Cabernet Franc. Sadly, Burr's health deteriorated as the vineyards thrived, and he passed away in 1993. But a comment he made in a documentary about Northern California wines reflected his thinking about the vital, even intimate relationship between grape grower and land: "The most important things in a vineyard are the footprints of the grower between the rows."

RAYMOND BURR VINEYARDS
8339 West Dry Creek Rd.
Healdsburg, CA 95448
707-433-4365
Rbwyn@aol.com
www.raymondburrvineyards.com

OWNER: Robert Benevides.

LOCATION: 8.5 miles west of Healdsburg via Dry Creek Rd. and Yoakim Bridge Rd.

APPELLATION: Dry Creek Valley.

HOURS: 11 A.M.–5 P.M. daily by appointment.

TASTINGS: Complimentary.

TOURS: None of winery.

THE WINES: Cabernet Franc, Cabernet Sauvignon, Chardonnay.

SPECIALTY: Hillside Vineyard Cabernet Sauvignon.

WINEMAKER: John Quinones.

ANNUAL PRODUCTION: 3,000 cases.

OF SPECIAL NOTE: Orchid greenhouse tours Saturdays and Sundays by appointment with minimum of 8 guests; picnic area with view of Dry Creek Valley; monthly food and wine tastings.

NEARBY ATTRACTIONS: Lake Sonoma (boating, camping, hiking).

SCHUG CARNEROS ESTATE WINERY

SCHUG CARNEROS ESTATE WINERY
602 Bonneau Rd.
Sonoma, CA 95476
707-939-9363
800-966-9365
schug@schugwinery.com
www.schugwinery.com

OWNERS: Walter and
Gertrud Schug.

LOCATION: .5 mile west of
intersection of Hwy. 121
and Hwy. 116.

APPELLATION: Carneros.

HOURS: 10 A.M.–5 P.M. daily.

TASTINGS: Complimentary;
$5 for reserve wines

TOURS: By appointment.

THE WINES: Cabernet
Sauvignon, Chardonnay,
Merlot, Pinot Noir,
Sauvignon Blanc, sparkling
wines.

SPECIALTY: Pinot Noir.

WINEMAKER: Michael Cox.

ANNUAL PRODUCTION: More
than 20,000 cases.

OF SPECIAL NOTE: Open
house in late April and in
mid-November (Holiday
in Carneros). *Pétanque*
court open to public.

NEARBY ATTRACTIONS:
Mission San Francisco
Solano and other historic
buildings in downtown
Sonoma; Vintage Aircraft
(scenic and aerobatic
biplane rides); Infineon
Raceway (auto racing);
Viansa Winery Wetlands
(tours).

og and wind from the Pacific Ocean and San Francisco Bay sweep along the low, rocky hills of the Carneros appellation, where the volcanic soil, laden with clay, is shallow and dense. Grape growers intent on producing Cabernet Sauvignon and many other premium varietals avoid these conditions at all costs. But Walter Schug wanted to grow Pinot Noir, and he knew that this challenging combination of climate and geology would bring out the best in his favorite grape.

Schug first made his reputation in the 1970s as the acclaimed winemaker for Joseph Phelps. Working at the ultrapremium Napa Valley winery, he was successful with a range of wine grapes, notably Cabernet Sauvignon, before turning his attention to Pinot Noir. In 1980, beginning with grapes from a vineyard he had used at Phelps, Schug launched his own brand.

Schug and his wife, Gertrud, selected a fifty-acre site in the southern Sonoma Valley for their new vineyard estate and crowned the hilltop with a winery in 1990. They favored post-and-beam architecture reminiscent of where the Schug family had The style makes it one of the wineries in the appellation. vineyards surround the winery, contracts with other growers best grapes year after year.

Germany's Rhine River Valley, long produced Pinot Noir. most instantly recognizable Pinot Noir and Chardonnay and Schug has long-term in the Carneros to ensure the Protecting and enhancing the varietal and regional characteristics of the fruit are the essence of the Schug family's philosophy.

The European aspect of the Schug estate was enhanced with the excavation of an underground cave system in the mid-1990s. The system's naturally stable temperatures and humidity levels allow the wines to age gracefully in French oak barrels. Almost every inch of the caves is covered with gray concrete, but an exposed patch at the end of one tunnel affords a glimpse of the pockmarked, pumicelike volcanic rock characteristic of the region.

Visitors are warmly welcomed at this family-managed winery. From the hilltop tasting room, they are treated to spectacular views of the surrounding countryside and the northern reaches of San Francisco Bay. Nearby is a *pétanque* court, another nod to the Schugs' European ancestry. Newcomers and old hands alike are encouraged to play this French game, which requires dexterity in tossing a small ball to exactly the right spot. More than merely a sport, *pétanque* is a pastime that invites conviviality and conversation in the best old-world tradition.

SEBASTIANI VINEYARDS AND WINERY

The Sebastianis have been growing grapes and making wine in Sonoma for nearly one hundred years. Over the decades, no other family name has been so inextricably linked to the Sonoma Valley's viticultural history. Artifacts from this storied past, such as carved wine barrels and old photographs, can be seen today at the family's remodeled winery in downtown Sonoma.

The Sebastiani story dates to 1895, when Samuele Sebastiani, a stonemason, emigrated from Tuscany to California, where he mined the hills of Sonoma for cobblestones that wound up on the streets of San Francisco. He used his hard-earned money to buy the oldest vineyards in Sonoma, which the Franciscan fathers had planted in 1825 to make sacramental wines. After Samuele's death in 1944, his son and daughter-in-law, August and Sylvia, bought the winery. August, acknowledged as one of the country's top winemakers of the day, shared his father's respect for craftsmanship, commissioning master woodcarver Earl Brown to hand-carve the now-famous Sebastiani barrels on display at the winery. August's widow and their children, Sam, Don, and Mary Ann, took the reins following his death in 1980.

The next two decades witnessed the company's greatest growth spurt as it built a large-volume portfolio of value brands that peaked at some 7 million cases a year, while still producing wine under the Sebastiani label. After the family decided to focus on premium grapes and the flagship brand, they sold the non-Sebastiani holdings. In the mid-1980s, Sam departed to start his own winery, Viansa, and in 2001, Don left to join Cecchetti Sebastiani Cellars. Mary Ann Sebastiani Cuneo then assumed the role of president and CEO.

Sebastiani Vineyards and Winery produces wine in four categories, including the Sonoma Proprietary and Estate Wine Selection, the company's signature luxury wine made from the Cherryblock estate vineyard. Located just north of the winery, Cherryblock was purchased in 1919 by Samuele Sebastiani, who planted a cherry orchard and grapevines, a traditional Italian combination. Today it consists of twenty-eight acres of Cabernet and a small amount of Merlot.

The Sebastianis are making wine in the same building that Samuele built from local field stone in 1903. In 2000, the family created a new hospitality center. The architects retained the structure's original Italian and Spanish mission character and added a curved, eighty-foot-long tasting bar, an art gallery, and a spacious retail shop. Adorning one wall is an impressive mural by Sonoma Valley artist Michael Wardel offering a bird's-eye view of the valley.

SEBASTIANI VINEYARDS AND WINERY
389 Fourth St. East
Sonoma, CA 95476
707-933-3200
info@sebastiani.com
www.sebastiani.com

OWNERS: Sebastiani and Cuneo families.

LOCATION: 4 blocks east of downtown Sonoma via East Spain St.

APPELLATION: Sonoma Valley.

HOURS: 10 A.M.–5 P.M. daily.

TASTINGS: $6–$10 for 3 wines; complimentary Chardonnay and dessert wine.

TOURS: Historical, Trolley, and Soil-to-Bottle tours and visits to Cherryblock vineyard by appointment.

THE WINES: Barbera, Cabernet Sauvignon, Chardonnay, Merlot, Mourvèdre, Pinot Noir, Sauvignon Blanc, Zinfandel.

SPECIALTY: Cherryblock Cabernet Sauvignon.

WINEMAKER: Mark Lyon.

ANNUAL PRODUCTION: 180,000 cases.

OF SPECIAL NOTE: Regular events such as book signings, cooking classes, and wine-and-food pairings; trellised picnic area beside vineyard and another shaded by trees; rotating exhibits by local artists. Shop featuring everything for the tabletop and estate olive oil and other condiments under the label of Sylvia, the family matriarch. Some wines have 2-bottle limits.

NEARBY ATTRACTIONS: Mission San Francisco Solano and other historic buildings in downtown Sonoma; Vella Cheese Company; Sonoma Cheese Factory; Train Town (rides for children); bike rentals.

SIMI WINERY

SIMI WINERY
16275 Healdsburg Ave.
Healdsburg, CA 95448
707-473-3231
www.simiwinery.com

OWNER: Franciscan Estates,
Fine Wine Division of
Constellation Brands.

LOCATION: 1 mile north of
Dry Creek Rd. exit off
U.S. 101, via Dry Creek Rd.

APPELLATION: Alexander
Valley.

HOURS: 10 A.M.–5 P.M. daily.

TASTINGS: $5 for 5 wines;
$7 for reserve wines.

TOURS: 11 A.M., 1 P.M., and
3 P.M. March–November;
11 A.M. and 2 P.M.
December–February.

THE WINES: Cabernet
Sauvignon, Chardonnay,
Merlot, Sauvignon Blanc,
Sendal (Sauvignon Blanc/
Semillon blend), Shiraz,
Zinfandel.

SPECIALTIES: Reserve
Chardonnay, Reserve
Cabernet Sauvignon.

WINEMAKER:
Nick Goldschmidt.

ANNUAL PRODUCTION:
140,000 cases.

OF SPECIAL NOTE: Barrel
Tasting Tuesdays include
barrel sampling along
with complimentary
winery tour.

NEARBY ATTRACTIONS:
Russian River (swimming,
canoe and kayak rentals).

A forest of redwoods shelters the entrance to this historic winery, which has been producing wines in the cellars here for more than a century. The parklike setting is enhanced by a babbling brook that runs between the visitor center and the winemaking facilities beyond it. Off to one side, picnic tables are set in the shade of a dozen or so of the towering trees, creating a cozy nook for enjoying a luncheon alfresco. Picnickers half expect Hansel and Gretel to wander by.

This area was considered remote when the winery was established by two Italian immigrants who found the rolling hills of the Alexander Valley reminiscent of their native Tuscany. Giusseppe and Pietro Simi had started making wine in San Francisco using Sonoma County grapes in 1876. The brothers relocated to Healdsburg five years later and began planting 126 acres of vineyards. The business prospered, and in 1890, they constructed a winery of basalt quarried from the surrounding countryside. The Simi brothers did not live long enough to witness the further success of their enterprise, which was taken over by Giusseppe's eighteen-year-old daughter, Isabelle, in 1904. An astute businesswoman, Isabelle sold all the winery's vineyard holdings at the beginning of Prohibition in 1920, a move that allowed her to maintain possession of cellared wines. When Prohibition was repealed at the end of 1933, she had a stash of some five hundred thousand perfectly cellared wines to sell to an eager public. In another brilliant stroke, she rolled out a twenty-five-thousand-gallon champagne cask and converted it into the winery's first tasting room in 1934. The redwoods were planted around the same time.

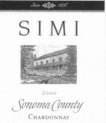

Descriptions of Simi's history, including Isabelle's struggles to keep the winery operating during Prohibition, are related during the regularly scheduled tours of the barrel cellars, winery, and the rest of the property. Old photographs and a handful of artifacts, such as a bottle of 1934 port, are on display in the tasting room. The historic room, remodeled in 1970, features a fireplace and a ceiling with a tentlike peak.

Over the decades, Simi Winery has acquired 535 acres in the Alexander Valley, most of which are devoted to red Bordeaux varieties. Another 100 acres in the nearby Russian River Valley, purchased in 1989, supply the winery's Chardonnay grapes. Called the Goldfields Vineyard, it produces a vineyard-designated Reserve Chardonnay. Simi made its first Alexander Valley vineyard-designated red wines in the harvest of 2000.

ST. FRANCIS WINERY & VINEYARDS

Sonoma Valley's history as the site of the last and northernmost of the Spanish missions established in California is reflected in the stunning architecture of the St. Francis Winery. The red tile–roofed, sand-colored stucco building, faithful to early mission style, has a two-story tower with a bell that is rung to mark every hour. A statue of St. Francis welcomes visitors to the new tasting room, where they are offered patio seating with breathtaking mountain and vineyard views. The visitor center opened in the spring of 2001, one mile west of the winery's former facility, completing the relocation of the entire operation. The new winery crowned thirty years of achievement by founder Joe Martin.

In 1971, the San Francisco businessman found himself in search of a change. He purchased the 1906 Behler Ranch in Kenwood and its hundred-acre vineyard, and began planting grapes that he sold to nearby wineries. The  following year, Martin was joined by his good friend, finance expert Lloyd Canton. Like many growers, the two eventually decided to build their own winery. St. Francis Winery, opened in 1979, is named after Saint Francis of Assisi, partly as a reference to the saint's role as a protector of animals and partly as an acknowledgment of the saint as a founder of the Franciscan order, which is credited with introducing European grape cultivation to the New World.

It is fitting that the one and only winemaker ever employed by St. Francis Winery & Vineyards was born and raised in San Francisco, a city also christened after the saint. Tom Mackey's arrival in 1983 ushered in a new direction at the winery: a heightened focus on red wines. When Mackey came on board, Martin and Canton added Cabernet Sauvignon and Zinfandel to the original mix of Chardonnay and Merlot. Over the next twenty years, St. Francis nurtured long-standing relationships with more than forty-five Sonoma County grape growers, which provided access to the Pagani Ranch and other enviable sources of old-vine Zinfandel grapes. Meanwhile, the winery developed more than five hundred acres of its own prime vineyards.

Among the wines previously produced from this diversity were Riesling, Gewürztraminer, Muscat, and Chardonnay, in addition to Merlot and Cabernet. Mackey gradually decreased the output of white wines from 80 percent when he came on board to 30 percent today, most of which is Chardonnay made from 100 percent Sonoma County grapes. With this change of focus to big, rich Cabernet, Merlot, and Zinfandel wines, St. Francis soon became known as "The House of Big Reds." Mackey has now created a series of small-lot single vineyard–designated wines available only at the visitor center.

ST. FRANCIS WINERY & VINEYARDS
100 Pythian Rd.
Santa Rosa, CA 95409
707-833-4666
800-543-7713
info@stfranciswine.com
www.stfranciswine.com

OWNERS: Joseph Martin and Lloyd Canton.

LOCATION: Off Hwy. 12, 6 miles east of Santa Rosa and 1 mile west of Kenwood.

APPELLATION: Sonoma Valley.

HOURS: 10 A.M.–5 P.M. daily.

TASTINGS: $5 for 4 wines.

TOURS: None.

THE WINES: Cabernet Sauvignon, Chardonnay, Merlot, Zinfandel.

SPECIALTIES: Reserve vineyard-designated Cabernet Sauvignon, Chardonnay, Merlot, Zinfandel.

WINEMAKER: Tom Mackey.

ANNUAL PRODUCTION: 250,000 cases.

OF SPECIAL NOTE: Single-vineyard wines sold only at winery. Annual events such as Barrel Tasting (March), Harvest in the Vineyards (September), Holiday Open House (November), and Festival of Lights (December). Elegant wine accessories at winery shop.

NEARBY ATTRACTIONS: Sugarloaf Ridge State Park (hiking, camping, horseback riding); Annadel State Park (hiking, biking).

STONE CREEK WINES

STONE CREEK WINES
9380 Hwy. 12
Kenwood, CA 95452
707-833-5070
info@stonecreekwines.com
www.stonecreekwines.com

OWNERS: Jacobs family.

LOCATION: About 10 miles
northwest of town of
Sonoma.

APPELLATION: Sonoma
Valley.

HOURS: 10:30 A.M.–5 P.M.
daily.

TASTINGS: Complimentary
for 4 wines.

TOURS: None.

THE WINES: Cabernet
Sauvignon, Chardonnay,
Merlot, Sauvignon Blanc,
White Zinfandel,
Zinfandel.

SPECIALTY: Merlot.

WINEMAKER: Erin Green.

ANNUAL PRODUCTION:
150,000 cases.

OF SPECIAL NOTE: Exclusive
Selection wines available
only at tasting room.
Picnic tables set on shaded
lawn. Condiments and
wine posters available at
gift shop.

NEARBY ATTRACTIONS:
Sugarloaf State Park
(hiking, camping,
horseback riding); Jack
London State Historic
Park (museum, hiking,
horseback riding);
Morton's Sonoma Springs
Resort (swimming,
picnicking).

The part of scenic state Highway 12 that passes through the town of Kenwood might well be called winery row. It is home to some of Sonoma County's major wineries, as well as several tasting rooms where visitors can familiarize themselves with wines they may be hearing of for the first time. Right on the highway in the heart of town is a cute clapboard house, painted blue and trimmed in white and maroon. This was Kenwood's one-room Old Blue Schoolhouse, built in 1872. By the 1930s, it had become a boardinghouse. Later it was a skating rink and a hardware store.

Today, the old schoolhouse is home to the Stone Creek Wines tasting room and offices. The company is owned by the Jacobs family, which has a colorful history. The family business dates to 1873, when patriarch Simon Levi established a general store in Southern California. Five generations followed in his footsteps, leading to the purchase of Stone Creek Wines in 1988.

Shaded by eucalyptus and evergreen trees, the building is fronted by a wide porch where two swings invite visitors to stay awhile. They are also welcome to bring along a picnic lunch, purchase some Stone Creek wine, and linger as long as they like on the shaded lawn. The entrance to the tasting room is through double oak doors with oval insets of glass etched with grapes and vines. The horseshoe-shaped tasting bar is to the left. Most visitors are

somewhat taken aback as they approach the counter and notice that an electric train is suspended on a track above the bar, going round and round all day.

Here, visitors receive complimentary tastes of Stone Creek's wines. There are three tiers from which to choose: the Stone Creek Chairman's Reserve and the Stone Creek Special Selection wines, as well as the more expensive Exclusive Selection wines, available only in the tasting room.

Stone Creek obtains its grapes from selected vineyards throughout California. The wines are then blended and nurtured to maturity by the winemaking team of Erin Green and Rebecca Martinsen. Green's relationship with the Jacobs family began in 1989 when she was employed at Vinwood Cellars, which at that time was storing and bottling the wine used by Stone Creek. The Jacobs family was so impressed with her winemaking skills that in 1995 they hired her as full-time winemaker. Her challenge is to create wines that are consistent and complex, yet among the least-expensive premium varietals of any made in California.

VIANSA WINERY & ITALIAN MARKETPLACE

Looking like a village in the Italian countryside, the terra-cotta villa and its grove of olive trees crown a knoll in the southern Sonoma Valley. If the spot reminds travelers of Tuscany, it's no surprise: Viansa proprietor Sam Sebastiani traces his ancestry to the region.

A member of the third generation of Sebastianis to make wine in Sonoma, Sam served as president of Sebastiani Vineyards from 1980 to 1986 and is generally credited with shifting the winery's emphasis from bulk wine to premium varietals. When he and his wife, Vicki, decided to establish their own winery, they saw an opportunity to distinguish themselves by focusing on Italian varietals and giving food equal billing. They chose to call their place Viansa, a combination of their first names. Sam's winemaking talents, Vicki's culinary expertise, and hundred-plus acres of estate vineyards proved to be a winning combination. Now a fourth generation is involved in the business: sons Jon and Michael serve on the board of directors, and son Joe is olive-oil estate and wetlands manager.

Viansa Winery, opened in 1990, produces the largest selection of Italian varietals of any American winery. In the early days, Viansa was known mostly for Chardonnay and Cabernet Sauvignon but has gradually increased its production of Italian wines from five thousand to fifty thousand cases a year. The two tasting bars in the Italian Marketplace pour samples of Italian varietals that have gained recognition in the United States, such as Sangiovese and Pinot Grigio, as well as less-familiar ones like Nebbiolo, Barbera, and Arneis. The marketplace is a mecca for food lovers who know they can find dozens of condiments, marinades, and sauces, samples of which are offered for impromptu tastings. For heartier fare, the *cucina* (Italian kitchen) prepares fresh salads, sandwiches, tortas, and desserts that can be taken out to one of the shaded picnic tables. From this perch, picnickers can enjoy the north-facing view of the Sonoma Valley, wedged between the Mayacamas Range to the east and the forested slopes of Sonoma Mountain to the west.

Directly north of the winery are ninety acres of lowlands that are flooded on a seasonal basis, rendering the site useless for grape growing. In 1992, Sam Sebastiani, a longtime conservationist and outdoorsman, began establishing a wetlands preserve that supports a variety of wildlife, including owls, egrets, tundra swans, golden eagles, Canada geese, and several species of ducks. More than 150 avian species have been spotted here, with more than 13,000 birds visiting each day during peak migratory periods in late winter and early spring. Sebastiani relishes knowing that he has provided valuable habitat by creating the county's largest privately owned, freshwater wetlands.

VIANSA WINERY & ITALIAN MARKETPLACE
25200 Arnold Dr.
Sonoma, CA 95476
707-935-4700
800-995-4740
tuscan@viansa.com
www.viansa.com

OWNERS: Sam and Vicki Sebastiani.

LOCATION: About 5 miles south of the town of Sonoma.

APPELLATION: Carneros.

HOURS: 10 A.M.–5 P.M. daily.

TASTINGS: Complimentary for 4 wines; $5 for 3 reserve wines.

TOURS: Guided tours of winery ($5) 11 A.M. and 2 P.M. daily; self-guided tours during operating hours. Two-hour wetlands tours ($15) on alternate Sundays, February–May.

THE WINES: Aleatico, Arneis, Barbera, Cabernet Franc, Cabernet Sauvignon, Chardonnay, Dolcetto, Freisa, Merlot, Moscata Grappa, Muscat Canelli, Nebbiolo, Pinot Grigio, Primitivo, Sangiovese, Sauvignon Blanc, Teroldego, Tocai Friulano, Vernaccia, Zinfandel.

SPECIALTIES: Italian varietals.

WINEMAKER: Sam Sebastiani.

ANNUAL PRODUCTION: 56,000 cases.

OF SPECIAL NOTE: Italian deli; outdoor barbecue in spring and summer. Cookbooks, condiments, and tabletop accessories at marketplace.

NEARBY ATTRACTIONS: Mission San Francisco Solano and other historic buildings in downtown Sonoma; Infineon Raceway (auto racing); Vintage Aircraft (scenic and aerobatic biplane rides).

MENDOCINO

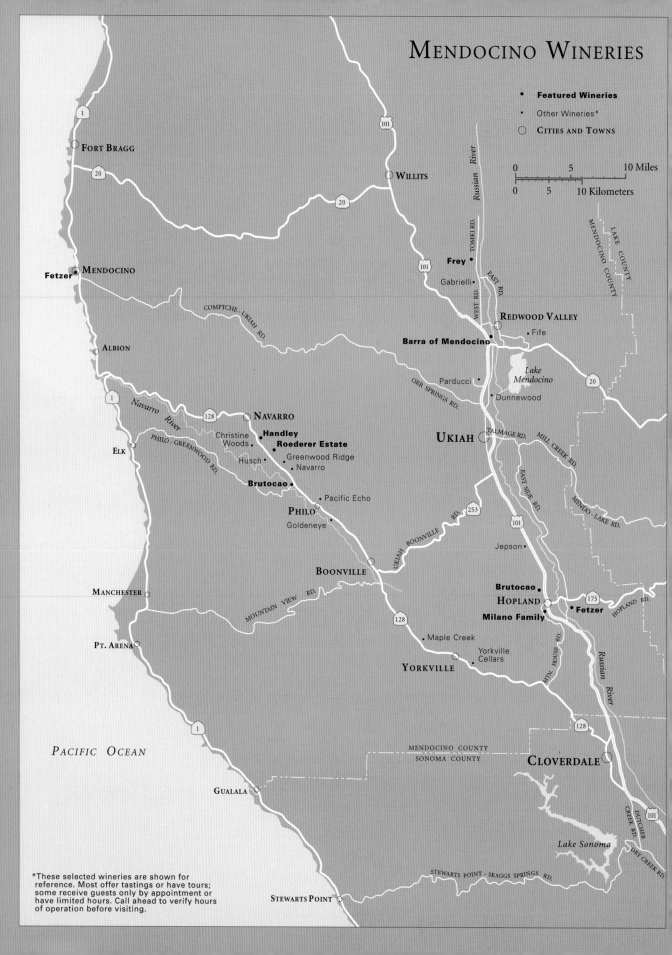

MENDOCINO WINERIES

- ● **Featured Wineries**
- • Other Wineries*
- ○ CITIES AND TOWNS

0   5   10 Miles

0   5   10 Kilometers

FORT BRAGG

WILLITS

Russian River

Frey
Gabrielli

MENDOCINO COUNTY
LAKE COUNTY

Fetzer MENDOCINO

REDWOOD VALLEY

Barra of Mendocino • Fife

COMPTCHE - UKIAH RD.

ALBION

Parducci
Lake Mendocino

ORR SPRINGS RD.

Dunnewood

Navarro River

NAVARRO

UKIAH

TALMAGE RD. MILL CREEK RD.

Christine Woods
Handley
Roederer Estate

ELK

Husch
Greenwood Ridge
• Navarro

EAST SIDE RD.

MENDO - LAKE RD.

PHILO - GREENWOOD RD.

Brutocao

Pacific Echo

PHILO

Goldeneye

UKIAH BOONVILLE RD.

253

Jepson

BOONVILLE

MANCHESTER

MOUNTAIN VIEW RD.

Brutocao
HOPLAND • Fetzer

Milano Family

HOPLAND RD.

175

PT. ARENA

128

Maple Creek

Yorkville Cellars

YORKVILLE

MTN. HOUSE RD.

Russian River

PACIFIC OCEAN

1

MENDOCINO COUNTY
SONOMA COUNTY

CLOVERDALE

128

GUALALA

DUTCHER CREEK RD.

DRY CREEK RD.

Lake Sonoma

STEWARTS POINT - SKAGGS SPRINGS RD.

STEWARTS POINT

*These selected wineries are shown for reference. Most offer tastings or have tours; some receive guests only by appointment or have limited hours. Call ahead to verify hours of operation before visiting.

I nland Mendocino has been slower to catch national attention than the county's dramatic coastline has, but that is changing as local winemakers prove that their grapes are on a par with those of Sonoma and Napa. There remains something of a pioneer spirit here, a love of the great outdoors that is reflected in a serious respect for the environment. It is no wonder that Mendocino leads the nation in farming organic vineyards.

Many Mendocino wineries are located off the beaten path in the shelter of redwoods or beside rivers. Most of the  county is undeveloped, a pristine landscape with abundant opportunities for hiking, fishing, camping, and other outdoor pursuits.

Wine grapes were first planted here in the middle of the nineteenth century, some by immigrants drawn to California by the 1849 Gold Rush. These farmers tended to plant food crops on the flat river plains and to position their vineyards on the more rugged hillsides and sun-exposed ridgetops. In time, they and their successors found fertile ground in the cooler Anderson Valley west of Hopland and Ukiah. The growing conditions vary so greatly between these two regions that Mendocino winemakers have found success with a wide spectrum of grape varietals.

BARRA OF MENDOCINO

I f the shape of this rural winery reminds you of something you can't quite put your finger on, try this: an inverted shallow champagne glass. The long stem is long gone, but otherwise the structure looks the way it was designed for the original owners, Weibel Champagne Cellars, in 1972. Charlie and Martha Barra do not make sparkling wines, but are known for a short, yet memorable list of still wines produced from organically grown grapes. The Barras get their grapes from their home ranch, Redwood Valley Vineyards (about two miles up the road), which is certified annually by the California Certified Organic Farmers (CCOF). The ranch's ten varieties provide a wide selection from which to choose should the Barras decide to expand their offerings. Charlie was born more than seventy-five years ago not far from his winery. He began pruning grapevines at

the age of nine and likes to say that his best high school graduation present was a pair of pruning shears. He's probably on his fiftieth pair by now, after more than that many harvests.

Mendocino County is in the forefront of organic grape growing, and Barra is in the forefront of Mendocino viticulture. In acknowledgment of his lifetime efforts, the Mendocino Winegrowers Alliance honored him at an awards dinner in 2002. In his acceptance speech, Barra said, "I am very honored. I take pride in being a good farmer, and a good steward of the land." It was that down-to-earth attitude that propelled him toward organic farming. Aware that chemical pesticides were endangering the long-term vitality of his land, Barra stopped using them in 1985. The grapes from the 175-acre Redwood Valley Vineyards are so highly regarded that they are sought out by premium wineries in Mendocino, Napa, and Sonoma Counties.

Like many other Mendocino grape growers, Barra was born to Italian immigrant parents accustomed to hard work in the vineyards. They were attracted to the area because of its resemblance to Italy's Piedmont region. As they farmed their new land, they were rewarded with a climate whose warm days and cool nights allow the grapes to mature at a slow pace, thus producing intense flavors.

Visitors to the tasting room at Redwood Valley Cellars find a large circular space with massive beams sweeping toward the ceiling and a fountain in the center. Outside, picnic tables can seat up to 180 people, and an expansive lawn and carefully tended garden encourage many of them to linger.

BARRA OF MENDOCINO
Tasting room at Redwood Valley Cellars
7051 North State St.
Redwood Valley, CA 95470
707-485-0322
RVV@pacific.net
www.barraofmendocino.com

OWNERS: Charles and Martha Barra.

LOCATION: 5 miles north of Ukiah via U.S. 101.

APPELLATION: Redwood Valley.

HOURS: 9:30 A.M.–5:30 P.M. daily.

TASTINGS: Complimentary.

TOURS: By appointment.

THE WINES: Cabernet Sauvignon, Muscat Canelli, Petite Sirah, Pinot Blanc, Pinot Noir.

SPECIALTY: Petite Sirah.

WINEMAKER: Various consulting winemakers.

ANNUAL PRODUCTION: 2,500 cases.

OF SPECIAL NOTE: Annual events include A Taste of Redwood Valley (June on Father's Day weekend), Sunset at the Cellars music festival (July), and wild mushroom gourmet dinners with guest chefs (November). Local pottery and art and Braren Pauli wines sold at tasting room.

NEARBY ATTRACTIONS: Real Goods Solar Living Center (tours, store); Lake Mendocino (hiking, boating, fishing, camping); Grace Hudson Museum (Pomo Indian baskets, historical photographs, changing art exhibits); Montgomery Woods (tallest redwood tree in world); Vichy Springs (mineral springs and resort).

BRUTOCAO CELLARS

BRUTOCAO CELLARS
13500 Hwy. 101
Hopland, CA 95449
800-433-3689

7000 Hwy. 128
Philo, CA 95466
707-895-2152

brutocao@pacific.net
www.brutocaocellars.com

OWNER: Leonard Brutocao.

LOCATION: U.S. 101 in downtown Hopland; Hwy. 128 in Anderson Valley.

APPELLATION: Mendocino.

HOURS: 10 A.M.–5 P.M. daily.

TASTINGS: Complimentary.

TOURS: By appointment.

THE WINES: Cabernet Sauvignon, Chardonnay, Merlot, Pinot Noir, Port, Sauvignon Blanc, Syrah, Zinfandel.

SPECIALTIES: Cabernet Sauvignon, Merlot, Zinfandel.

WINEMAKER: Fred Nickel.

ANNUAL PRODUCTION: 12,000 cases.

OF SPECIAL NOTE: Port and Syrah available only at tasting rooms. Crushed Grape Restaurant serving pizza and California cuisine. Annual events include Cioppino Feed Bocce Tourney (April), Hopland Passport (April and October), Anderson Valley Pinot Noir Festival (May), Lavender Festival (June), Big Bottles and Bocce BBQ (June), Brutocao Wine Country Bocce Classic (September), Port and Chocolate Tasting (November).

NEARBY ATTRACTIONS: Real Goods Solar Living Center (tours, store); Fetzer Organic Gardens (tours); Sho-Ka-Wah Casino; Hendy Woods State Park (redwood groves, hiking, camping).

Downtown Hopland was a quiet place with only a hotel, two modest restaurants, a brew pub, and the odd antique shop until the Brutocao family came to town. The Brutocaos, who had been making wine under their own label and already operated a tasting room in nearby Anderson Valley, decided to establish a presence on U.S. 101. In 1997, Brutocao Cellars purchased the old Hopland High School from the Fetzer wine family and began creating a seven-and-a-half-acre complex dedicated to food and wine. Schoolhouse Plaza opened two years later with a tasting room, a gift shop, and the Crushed Grape Restaurant in the remodeled 1920s building, which still has its original façade bearing the high school's name. On display in the tasting room and restaurant are memorabilia from the school's glory days.

The Brutocaos, who trace their heritage to Italy, brought more than a love of food and wine when they came to this country. They are also passionate about bocce ball, a devilishly challenging game with a half-century Italian lineage. The complex has six regulation bocce (pronounced BOTCH-ee) courts, which are lighted and open to the public.

With the remodeling complete, the winery set to work landscaping the grounds with some six thousand lavender plants and thirty-four hundred rosebushes. More than half of the roses are in eighteen terraced rows that create a rainbow of pinks, whites, and yellows. The gardens reach their peak in June but provide beauty from early May through November. Between the terraces and the bocce ball courts is an expanse of manicured lawn with a peaked-roof gazebo that is used for weddings and other special events.

Brutocao Cellars is a tale of two families who combined their skills and expertise to establish one of Mendocino County's most notable wineries. The Brutocaos immigrated from Venice in the early 1900s, bringing with them a passion for wine. Len Brutocao met Marty Bliss while in school at Berkeley. Marty's father, Irv, had been farming land in Mendocino since the 1940s. Len and Marty married, and soon thereafter the families joined forces and began to grow grapes. The family sold their grapes to other wineries for years before starting to make their own wine in 1991. They selected the Lion of St. Mark from St. Mark's Cathedral in Venice as their symbol of family tradition and quality. The heart of that quality, they say, is in their 575 acres of vineyards in southern Mendocino County and another 12 acres (of Pinot Noir) in Anderson Valley. The original tasting room in Philo is still in use. With its high-beamed ceilings and wisteria-covered patio, it makes an ideal stop for those traveling scenic Highway 128 to the Pacific Coast.

FETZER VINEYARDS

In essence, growing grapes is an agricultural endeavor, requiring the same kind of expertise, perseverance, and responsible farming practices as any other crop. Nowhere is the link between successful grape growing and respect for the environment more evident than at the Fetzer Vineyards Valley Oaks Ranch in scenic southern Mendocino County.

The Fetzer family has spent more than twenty years improving the winery's energy efficiency and vineyard practices, and the sustainability of its general business operations. In addition to composting and recycling, Fetzer is the only winery in the United States to have its oak barrels built on-site and to operate an in-house  oak-barrel restoration program that adds years to the life of a wine barrel. Most importantly, Fetzer has become an industry leader in farming grapes organically. It also has encouraged other growers to adopt similar practices and has supported them in their efforts by sharing information and expertise.

At the same time, Fetzer pursues a winemaker's ultimate goal: the production of high-quality wines that are popular and critical successes. The winery's premium varietals, Five Rivers Ranch and Barrel Select wines, and Reserve Collection have won top awards at national and international competitions.

The wines are only one of many reasons to visit the ninety-five-acre Valley Oaks Ranch. While many wineries support the idea of linking wine with food, Fetzer has taken the concept to its logical extension by planting an extensive organic garden of fruits, vegetables, and herbs, along with flowers. Within the five acres, visitors find a number of special gardens with clearly labeled plants. In the Mediterranean Walk, a canopy of pomegranates, figs, and olives shelters aromatic herbs and other plants. A gazebo and a fountain provide focal points in the Reserve Garden of roses and wisteria. In the Border of Life are flowers that attract hummingbirds and butterflies as well as beneficial insects. Strolling through these lush and prolific gardens—either independently or with Garden Director Kate Frey—gives visitors vivid and memorable impressions of the sustainable growing practices in use throughout the Fetzer properties. It's also permissible to carry a glass of wine along for some on-the-spot pairings with fruits and vegetables. If that leaves visitors hungry, they can purchase sandwiches, salads, or pastas in the spacious Garden Café, which also houses the tasting room.

Along with special in-depth garden seminars and demonstrations, Fetzer offers cooking classes and food-and-wine events led by Culinary Director John Ash, an internationally recognized chef, educator, and author.

FETZER VINEYARDS
13601 East Side Rd.
Hopland, CA 95449
707-744-1250
800-846-8637
www.fetzer.com

OWNER: Brown-Forman Corporation.

LOCATION: 1 mile east of U.S. 101 in Hopland via Hwy. 175.

APPELLATION: Mendocino.

HOURS: 9 A.M.–5 P.M. daily.

TASTINGS: Complimentary tastings of Fetzer wines and Bonterra organically grown wines from a sister winery.

TOURS: Tours of garden three times daily May–September.

THE WINES: Cabernet Sauvignon, Chardonnay, Gewürztraminer, Johannisberg Riesling, Merlot, Pinot Noir, Sauvignon Blanc, Syrah, White Zinfandel, Zinfandel.

SPECIALTIES: Reserve Collection, Five Rivers Ranch wines.

WINEMAKER: Dennis Martin.

ANNUAL PRODUCTION: 4 million cases.

OF SPECIAL NOTE: 10-room bed-and-breakfast inn. Special garden and culinary events and demonstrations throughout year. Heirloom seeds, oils and vinegars flavored with organic herbs from Fetzer's garden, and gourmet foods sold at winery. Picnic tables provided. Second tasting room at 45070 Main St. in village of Mendocino.

NEARBY ATTRACTIONS: Real Goods Solar Living Center (tours, store); Sho-Ka-Wah Casino; Vichy Springs (mineral springs and resort).

FREY VINEYARDS, LTD.

FREY VINEYARDS, LTD.
14000 Tomki Rd.
Redwood Valley, CA 95470
707-485-5177
800-760-3739
frey@saber.net
www.freywine.com

OWNERS: Frey family.

LOCATION: 7 miles north of Ukiah off U.S. 101.

APPELLATION: Redwood Valley.

HOURS: By appointment.

TASTINGS: Complimentary.

TOURS: By appointment.

THE WINES: Cabernet Sauvignon, Chardonnay, Gewürztraminer, Merlot, Petite Sirah, Pinot Noir, Sangiovese, Sauvignon Blanc, Syrah, Zinfandel.

SPECIALTIES: Certified organic wines without added sulfites; biodynamically grown estate-bottled wines.

WINEMAKERS: Paul and Jonathan Frey.

ANNUAL PRODUCTION: 40,000 cases.

OF SPECIAL NOTE: Picnic area for visitors' use; biodynamic herbal tinctures made from vineyard-grown herbs sold at winery.

NEARBY ATTRACTIONS: Real Goods Solar Living Center (tours, store); Lake Mendocino (hiking, boating, fishing, camping); Grace Hudson Museum (Pomo Indian baskets, historical photographs, changing art exhibits); Sho-Ka-Wah Casino; Vichy Springs (mineral springs and resort); Orr Hot Springs (mineral springs spa).

Arguably the most low-key winery in California, this gem is hidden off a two-lane road that wends through an undeveloped corner of Redwood Valley. Unsuspecting visitors might mistake the first building for the tasting room, but that's grandma's house. They must drive past it to reach the winery, and upon arriving, they find that there is no formal tasting room. Instead, tastings are conducted outdoors at a couple of planks set over a pair of wine barrels. When temperatures drop or rain falls, everyone retires to the original house—a redwood structure fashioned from an old barn—where the senior Mrs. Frey lives. Visitors are encouraged to picnic at one of several redwood tables and benches hand-hewn by the late family patriarch, Paul.

Virtually everything at this winery seems handmade or fashioned from something else. Barrels and tanks have been salvaged from larger operations, and the winery itself was constructed of redwood from a defunct winery  in Ukiah. Some rows of grapevines are interplanted with herbs such as echinacea and valerian, which are harvested and extracted into herbal essences.

Frey (pronounced fry) Vineyards is the oldest and largest all-organic winery in the United States. It may have another claim to fame as the winery with the most family members on the payroll. In 1961, Paul and Marguerite Frey, both doctors, bought ninety-nine acres near the headwaters of the Russian River. The Redwood Valley property seemed a great place to raise a family. Five of the couple's twelve children were born after the move, and most are still in the neighborhood.

In 1965, the Freys planted forty acres of Cabernet Sauvignon and Grey Riesling grapevines on the ranch's old pastureland, but they didn't start making wine until the 1970s. Eldest son Jonathan, who studied organic viticulture, began tending the vineyards and harvesting the grapes, which at first were sold to other wineries. When a Cabernet Sauvignon made with their grapes won a gold medal for a Santa Cruz winery, the family realized the vineyard's potential. Frey Vineyards was founded the next year, in 1980.

In 1996, the family began farming biodynamically. The word *biodynamic* stems from the agricultural theories of Austrian scientist and educator Rudolf Steiner. Biodynamic practices undertake to restore vitality to the soil. The farm is managed as a self-sustaining ecosystem, using special composting methods and specific planting times. As good stewards of the land, Frey started the first organic winery and is now the only American winery fully certified by Demeter, the biodynamic certification organization. The wines have won many gold and silver medals for excellence.

HANDLEY CELLARS

On entering the Handley Cellars tasting room in the western Anderson Valley, many visitors do a double take when they see Oaxacan carvings, African textiles, and other crafts from around the world. But the eye eventually settles on the English pub–style bar. Then visitors know they are in the right place. Winery co-owner Milla Handley came naturally to her interest in both crafts and wine. She was an art major before she embarked on her winemaking career at the University of California at Davis, and her father, Raymond, is the proprietor of Xanadu, which specializes in ethnographic art. Milla Handley's career choice also might have been dictated by genetics. She is the great-great-granddaughter of the famous brewer Henry Weinhard.

After working for three years at Chateau St. Jean, Handley relocated to the Anderson Valley with her husband, Rex McClellan. She joined nearby Edmeades Winery in 1979 before she and her husband started their own winery in the basement of their home in 1982.  Her goal was to make Chardonnay that reflected her personal taste. The winery's first release, the 1982 North Coast Chardonnay, won a gold medal at the prestigious Orange County Fair. The couple built their current winery in 1986.

Some of the Handley vineyards are visible from the tasting room. The winery owns sixty acres of the old Holmes Ranch, half of which is planted with grapevines. Three original outbuildings remain on the property. One is the restored ranch house, which is used for private entertaining. An old barn holds vineyard equipment. Between the two is the photogenic water tower. Photographs displayed in the tasting room show the ranch and nearby towns as they looked decades ago.

Handley is the westernmost winery in the Anderson Valley. The seventeen-mile drive from there to the Mendocino coast is one of the most scenic stretches of Highway 128. A colorful aspect of regional history is the local lingo, Boontling. This unique language, created by residents of nearby Boonville in the 1880s, confounded anyone from outside the town limits. Just for fun, Handley has named its White Riesling/Gewürztraminer blend Brightlighter, Boontling for "city folk."

On all but the stormiest of days, the best place to sit and sip is in the courtyard shaded by trees and a trellis of wisteria that rains purple petals in spring. When they cease, the scent of lavender wafts through this serene outdoor room. Stone statues, ancient stone carvings, and a bronze temple lion provide elegant company.

HANDLEY CELLARS
3151 Hwy. 128
Philo, CA 95466
707-895-3876
800-733-3151
info@handleycellars.com
www.handleycellars.com

OWNERS: Milla Handley, Rex McClellan, and Raymond Handley.

LOCATION: About 6 miles northwest of Philo.

APPELLATION: Anderson Valley.

HOURS: 11 A.M.–5 P.M. daily; until 6 P.M. May–October.

TASTINGS: Complimentary.

TOURS: By appointment.

THE WINES: Blanc de Blancs, Brightlighter White (Gewürztraminer/White Riesling blend), Brut, Brut Rosé, Chardonnay, Gewürztraminer, Pinot Gris, Pinot Noir, Sauvignon Blanc, Zinfandel.

SPECIALTIES: Chardonnay, Gewürztraminer, Pinot Noir.

WINEMAKERS: Milla Handley and Denny Dudzik.

ANNUAL PRODUCTION: 12,000–14,000 cases.

OF SPECIAL NOTE: Food and wine pairings on first weekend of each month. Annual events include Expressions of Anderson Valley (July). International folk art and crafts sold at winery.

NEARBY ATTRACTIONS: Hendy Woods State Park (redwood groves, hiking, camping).

MILANO FAMILY WINERY

MILANO FAMILY WINERY
14594 South Hwy. 101
Hopland, CA 95449
707-744-1396
wines@milanowinery.com
www.milanowinery.com

OWNERS: Ted and Deanna Starr.

LOCATION: About .5 mile south of Hopland.

APPELLATION: Mendocino.

HOURS: 10 A.M.–5 P.M. daily.

TASTINGS: Complimentary; $5 for reserve wines.

TOURS: By appointment.

THE WINES: Cabernet Sauvignon, Carignane, Chardonnay, Echo and Sanel (Bordeaux blends), Port, Sunshine (French Colombard/Muscat blend), Syrah, Zinfandel.

SPECIALTIES: Cabernet Sauvignon, Port, Zinfandel.

WINEMAKER: Deanna Starr.

ANNUAL PRODUCTION: 6,000 cases.

OF SPECIAL NOTE: Small percentage of wines distributed outside winery; bottle limits on library wines. Events include Hopland Passport (April and October) and frequent concerts at the winery.

NEARBY ATTRACTIONS: Fetzer Organic Gardens (tours); Sho-Ka-Wah Casino; Vichy Springs (mineral springs and resort); Real Goods Solar Living Center (tours, store).

What looks like a big, old barnlike structure set back from the highway was built in 1947 not as a winery but as a hop kiln. The building is just south of downtown Hopland, which got its name from the period—late 1800s through mid-1900s—when the growing and processing of hops were important industries in Mendocino County. The dried cones of the hop flowers are a major ingredient in beer.

The hop business was still booming in the 1940s when Vincenzo Milone and his son, Frank, who had been farming pears, prunes, and grapes as well as hops on the surrounding acres, decided to replace a kiln burned down in the late 1930s by a moonshiner. In 1954, when the demand for local hops died out, the facility closed its doors. Twenty-two years later, Vincenzo's grandson, Jim, transformed the old kiln into a winery, the Milano Family Winery. The current owners, Deanna and Ted Starr, bought the winery in 2001. The couple had their own busi-nesses in Southern California and were visiting acquaintances in near-by Sonoma when they heard of a winery for sale in an unfamiliar place called Hopland. They drove up to see it and fell in love with the old build-ing, the town, and the rolling hills dotted with oak trees. They found it surprisingly easy to give up their hurried life for rustic Mendocino County.

The Starrs are happy to show visitors how hops were originally processed, along with the current winemaking activities. The structure is one of only three hop kilns remaining in the county and the only one open to the public. Visitors who climb the exterior staircase of the old kiln to the second-floor tasting room are in for a treat, not only because of the wine. The entire room, including the bar, is made of heart redwood. The tall tasting bar is the perfect height to rest your elbows on as you begin to unwind while sipping one of Milano's handmade wine selections.

The former owners produced up to thirty-five thousand cases of wine a year, but the Starrs plan to keep production at about six thousand cases so special care can be given to every barrel. Ted, a software developer for the past several years, has created a program to manage tasting rooms, wine clubs, and inventory. Winemaker Deanna's background is in nursing and home health administra-tion, but her hobby is gourmet cooking. As she notes, her nursing knowledge has helped her understand the chemistry of winemaking, and her cooking experience has taught her about balancing flavors. Visitors often buy a bottle to enjoy at picnic tables set in the shade of a trellis, where they have views of the Sanel Valley. Sometimes they linger to visit with Morgan the pony and Buster the donkey in the horse pasture and keep an eye out for the pair of pygmy goats, Spic and Span.

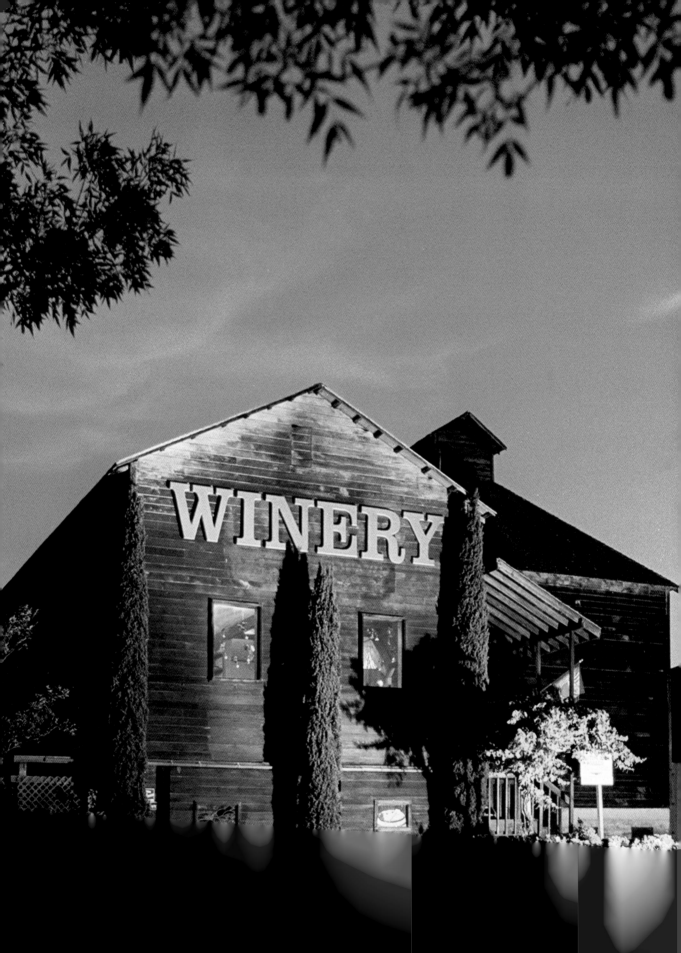

ROEDERER ESTATE

Roederer Estate is nestled in the cool, fog-shrouded Anderson Valley, where the climate and well-drained soils provide the ideal growing conditions for sparkling wine grapes. The estate's wines are made in the French style—by the *méthode champenoise*—an elaborate process whereby the wine is fermented for the second time in the actual bottle rather than in a tank. Although this type of fermentation takes longer, it produces a superior sparkling wine. Nothing less would be expected from this winery, whose parent company, Champagne Louis Roederer, has been in business in Reims, France, since 1776.

And as befits a winery in the southwest corner of Mendocino's Anderson Valley, the winery is made of redwood, instead of stone as is common in France. The facility, at forty-eight thousand square feet, does not look as large as it sounds. It is discreetly built into the hill, with large cellars set below ground level. The lawn is rimmed by a border of hardy perennials including agapanthus, daylilies, roses,  yarrow, penstemon, and other varieties that provide lavender, yellow, pink, and red blossoms during much of the year.

The landscaping as well as the forested ridges to the west are clearly visible through large windows in the tasting room. An ornately carved ten-foot-tall antique armoire dominates the entrance. The other décor suggests the hand of someone French: there is plenty to amuse the eye but not so much that the space looks cluttered. An elegant tasting bar hand-carved of black walnut runs the length of one side of the room. On the opposite wall hangs a row of nine large prints of Emile Bourdelin wood carvings. The originals, commissioned by Louis Roederer, depict winery scenes from the early 1900s. Chairs and square tables are arrayed beneath the prints. At the far end of the room, a carefully selected collection of potted palms completes the effect of a Parisian bistro. Even the floor tiles are French. Red and as thick as bricks, they were made in the mid-eighteenth century and once graced a chateau in the old country.

Roederer Estate is a family-owned company whose owner, president Jean-Claude Rouzaud, is a fifth-generation descendant of the founder. He carefully selected the site of the winery, which comprises 480 acres of vineyards. About 60 percent of the acreage is planted in Chardonnay grapes, and the remainder, in Pinot Noir.

ROEDERER ESTATE
4501 Hwy. 128
Philo, CA 95466
707-895-2288
info@roedererestate.net
www.roederer-estate.com

OWNERS: Champagne Louis Roederer/Jean-Claude Rouzaud.

LOCATION: About 6 miles northwest of Philo.

APPELLATION: Anderson Valley.

HOURS: 11 A.M.–5 P.M. daily.

TASTINGS: $3 for 5 or 6 wines.

TOURS: By appointment.

THE WINES: Brut, Brut Rosé, L'Ermitage, Pinot Noir.

SPECIALTY: L'Ermitage.

WINEMAKER: Michel J. Salgues.

ANNUAL PRODUCTION: 60,000–70,000 cases.

OF SPECIAL NOTE: Pinot Noir and jeroboams (3-liter bottles) of Brut and Brut Rosé sparkling wines available only at winery. Annual Anderson Valley Pinot Noir Festival (May).

NEARBY ATTRACTIONS: Hendy Woods State Park (redwood groves, hiking, camping).

Wine House Press
127 East Napa Street, Suite F
Sonoma, CA 95476
707-996-1741

Editor and publisher: Tom Silberkleit
Cover and interior design: Jennifer Barry Design, Fairfax, CA
Layout production: Kristen Wurz
Copyeditor: Judith Dunham
Maps: Ben Pease
Proofreader: Linda Bouchard

All photographs by Robert Holmes except the following: page 24, bottom left:
Lenny Siegel Photographic; page 26: Kate Kline May; page 27: John Sutton; pages 32 and 33: Avis Mandel;
page 43, bottom right: © Charles Feil, 2001, viewsfromabove.com; page 48, bottom right:
Gundolf Pfotenhauer; page 51, bottom left: Avis Mandel; pages 62 and 63: creativedirections.com; page 112,
bottom right: Pradoe Advertising and Design; page 116, bottom left: Avis Mandel; page 117:
Avis Mandel; pages 132 and 133: John Birchard; page 139: Charles Starr.

Front cover photograph: Fetzer Vineyards
Back cover photographs: top left: St. Clement Vineyards (Robert Holmes);
top right: Franciscan Oakville Estate (Avis Mandel); bottom left: Robert Mondavi Winery (Robert Holmes);
bottom right: Mumm Napa Valley (Robert Holmes).

Printed and bound in Singapore through Dai Nippon Printing America, LLC

ISBN 0-9724993-1-8

First Edition, Second Printing

Distributed by Ten Speed Press, P.O. Box 7123, Berkeley, CA 94707, www.tenspeed.com

The publisher has made every effort to ensure the accuracy of the information contained in
The California Directory of Fine Wineries, but can accept no liability for any loss, injury, or inconvenience
sustained by any visitor as a result of any information or recommendation contained in this guide.
Travelers should always call ahead to confirm hours of operation, fees, and other highly variable information.

Always act responsibly when drinking alcoholic beverages by selecting a designated driver
or prearranged transportation.

Customized Editions
Wine House Press will print custom editions of this volume for bulk purchase at your request.
Personalized covers and foil-embossed corporate logo imprints can be created in large quantities for
special promotions or events, or as premiums. For more information, contact Custom Imprints,
Wine House Press, 127 E. Napa Street, Suite F, Sonoma, CA 95476; 707-996-1741.

ACKNOWLEDGMENTS

Books, like films and plays, are the result of a multiplicity of carefully orchestrated factors. Creativity, perseverance, and commitment all have important roles in guaranteeing the success of a project. The artistic and editorial team who worked on this book possesses these qualities in large measures. My heartfelt thanks go to the following professionals who gave the best of themselves: Marty Olmstead, writer; Robert Holmes, photographer; Jennifer Barry, designer; Judith Dunham, copyeditor; Linda Bouchard, proofreader; Ben Pease, cartographer; and Kristen Wurz, layout production.

In addition, I am most grateful for the invaluable counsel of Barbara Moulton, Marc Mezzetta, and Greg Taylor; my editorial advisor and late-night crisis administrator, Danny Biederman; the staff of Readers' Books; and the gentle spirits of Chester and Francis Arnold, whose early guidance and artistic instincts helped propel this project forward.

Special thanks must go to my father, William Silberkleit, to whom I owe a lifelong debt. By his example, I have come to realize that persistence and hard work are the keys to unlocking lofty goals. I am also forever grateful to Estelle Silberkleit, a mother whose eyes and ears have always been open to new ideas and untried literary projects. And finally, for putting up with work-filled weekends and midnight deadlines for many months, my apologies, thank-yous, and enduring affection go to Gent and Lisa Silberkleit.

—Tom Silberkleit